THE WORD

THE WORD

Imagining the Gospel in Modern America

Ann Monroe

Westminster John Knox Press
Louisville, Kentucky

Book design by Sharon Adams

First edition
Published by Westminster John Knox Press
Louisville, Kentucky

This book is printed on acid-free paper that meets the American National Standards Institute Z39.48 standard. ♾

PRINTED IN THE UNITED STATES OF AMERICA

00 01 02 03 04 05 06 07 08 09 — 10 9 8 7 6 5 4 3 2 1

Library of Congress Cataloging-in-Publication Data is on file at the Library of Congress, Washington, D. C.

ISBN 0-664-22141-6

Contents

Acknowledgments

No book is written by its author alone. My thanks are due first of all to the dozens of people who invited me into their churches, their Bible studies, and their lives. Without their openhearted welcome, this book would not exist.

Many people helped me work through the issues that arose in my reporting whose contributions are not immediately evident in the pages that follow. I am indebted to Burt Visotsky (from whose book *Reading the Book* my midrash examples are taken) for his patient guidance through the thickets of midrash, and to Anne Richards and Paul Steinke for a chance to look at paintings I otherwise would not have seen. I also want to thank David Morgan, Mark Powell, Barbara Wheeler, Mark Sisk, Bill Countryman, Susan Schaeffer, Tom Gallagher, Carl Boyer, Dan Ade, Verna Dozier, Emmett Jarrett, Joe Shank, Steve Todd, Sharon Ringe, Vesta Kowalski, David, Lucia and Jessie Webster, and Paul Gordon Chandler for conversations, insights, and all-around help.

Kerry Tremain, Patti Wolter, and Marilyn Snell at *Mother Jones,* and Bob Hulteen, at *Sojourners,* gave me the chance to start asking the questions that led to this book. Mary Driscoll knows how much I owe her. Nick Street, at Westminster John Knox, has been everything a writer could hope an editor would be.

Lucy, Rick, and Jason Shick matched their hospitality with their enthusiasm for the project; my husband John and son Josh encouraged me, nagged me when I flagged, and patiently put up with my frequent absences, both physical and psychological.

My deepest thanks go to the St. Luke's Monday night Bible study, the community in which, and from which, I have learned most of what I know about reading this book; and to Roger Ferlo, who has played the triple role of pastor, sounding board, and subject with grace and generosity. To him, and to all the members of the Monday night Bible study, past and present, this book is dedicated.

Preface

I was not brought up reading the Bible; I didn't begin reading it regularly until well into my adulthood. And when I did, I wasn't a bit sure I liked it. "It doesn't feel very *religious*," I remember complaining to the priest who had urged me to start the practice.

I've been reading the book ever since, both on my own, and—more rewardingly—in a series of different Bible study groups. Some were led by experts in biblical criticism; others by just plain folks. Some had no leaders at all. Some have been culturally homogeneous, and some have been anything but.

After years of this, I'm still not sure I *like* the Bible. But whether I like it or not has become increasingly less the point. The Bible has gotten its hooks into me.

This book is an attempt to figure out something about what it is that we do—I and the multitude of other Bible readers in this country—when we say we read the Bible. At first glance, reading the Bible might seem a simple activity. But the Bible is not something we ordinarily pick up, on a free afternoon, to kill a little time. Whether we are religious or not, the Bible carries a lot of freight: the massive literary, historical, spiritual, and theological freight between its covers and an enormous amount of cultural baggage to boot. To choose to read it involves an inner gearing-up, like a hawk gathering itself for a dive.

I am a reporter; I watch things happen, ask questions, then write about what I watched and learned. That's what I've done in this book. I've watched people teach the Bible, study it, wrestle with it. I've talked to them about how they feel about the book, how they handle it, what they think it is. I have focused primarily on the Christian Bible not because I discount the Jewish scriptures but because it is in its Christian form that the Bible has tended most often to command the American imagination. And I have focused on religious readers of the Bible—as opposed to readers with a strictly literary or intellectual interest in it—because it is their readings that are the most charged and contentious.

This book is what I have made of it all. It is anything but comprehensive. As I've worked on it, I've often felt as though I was surveying a huge landscape, at night, by flashes of lightning. There is much more that I do not know than that I do, much more that I have not seen than that I have. I have had to make arbitrary choices about where to go and whom to talk to, and sometimes I have simply gone where my life was taking me anyhow. A lot of sheer chance has gone into this book—chance that has often shaded into serendipity.

The reason for doing it? That despite the complaint, which I heard often in my reporting, that America is becoming biblically illiterate, the Bible has huge power in this country, both among those who read it and among those who don't. As I write, *The New York Times* gave prominent coverage to a new computer game called "The War in Heaven"—coverage the game wouldn't have gotten, I'd guess, if it were merely violent, and not (as it is) Christian and violent. Since I started reporting this book, the Bible has hit the front covers of all three national newsweeklies.

Throughout my reporting, I kept returning to the touchstone question: What do we mean when we say we read the Bible? Pollsters ask whether their subjects read the Bible as part of their religious practice, and sociologists wield the poll results, as though the simple fact that a person reads the Bible says something clear and distinct about him or her—as though the five or six people you sometimes see in a New York City subway car with this book open on their laps were in some way defined by that fact and no other. They are reading the Bible; what else do you need to know? I have sometimes read the Bible on the subway too, and I have felt defined by the glances, whether approving or disapproving, of other passengers. Since I know that I am not defined, solely, by the fact that I read the Bible, I figure the same is true of other Bible readers: that they come to it for different reasons, in different ways, and out of different imaginative pictures of its role in their lives. Reading the Bible is not a cookie-cutter activity.

As I've worked on this book, I've become more and more convinced that how Americans read the Bible is both a more complicated and a more interesting subject than either the news media or the pollsters generally give it credit for being. Whether or not I am right in this conviction, I leave to the reader to determine.

A note about sourcing: All of my interviews were on the record. But because I believe it's unfair to strip people of their religious privacy—of any privacy, for that matter—without their consent, I promised anonymity to the members of the Bible studies I visited unless they agreed to the use of their names. For that reason, the names of many Bible study participants in this book have been changed. A few names were also changed simply to avoid duplication. To make the accounts of the Bible studies easier to follow, I have sometimes combined two or more participants into one. I have not, however, changed or invented any part of the discussions themselves.

Chapter 1

The Lay of the Land

Tampa, FL; San Francisco, CA; New York, NY

I. BILLY GRAHAM REVIVAL

Tampa, FL

The Tampa Bay Stadium is surrounded by buses, most of them labeled with the name of the church they have come from. It's not the lost sheep who come to hear Billy Graham. It's people who already go to church.

The buzz in the stadium is that this is Billy's last revival, and that he wanted to hold it here because this is where he went to Bible school. This is where he was converted, on a golf course where he'd gone for a long walk. He knelt on the 18th hole and said, "God, I know you are calling me, but you have to help. I can't do it myself."

Actually, as he tells the story, he says, "I cain't do it myself." It's part of what makes him appealing, the odd juxtaposition of leonine profile and country-boy twang.

Behind me, a man is dissing his church Bible study. "It's so academic," he says, "and this is so real."

Last night in my motel room I watched a TV news reporter interview a black man who'd come down onto the stadium floor to be saved on the first night of the crusade. Looking around

1

tonight, I wonder cynically how hard they had to look to find him. It's a sea of white faces.

We are being entertained with Christian light rock and slick videos and a really dynamite country fiddler, whose "I'll Fly Away" gets even my reluctant toes tapping. "God sent us an angel today," says one singer, asking us to stand, hold hands, and pray.

As the final run-up to Billy himself, his longtime lead entertainer, George Beverly Shea, gives us an emotion-filled rendition of "That Old Rugged Cross." A group of teenagers across the aisle sniggers in embarrassment.

Billy Graham enters to a standing ovation.

He is an old man now, and he speaks more in sorrow than in anger of the broad road that leads to destruction, judgment, and hell, and of the narrow road that leads to heaven and paradise.

"Crucifixion is the most terrible of all deaths," he says. "Jesus was beaten with leather thongs with metal pellets on them; he had a crown of thorns jammed onto his head and carried a heavy wooden cross. He was weakened by loss of blood, and the crowds were jeering at him. When they pulled his beard, his face bled. God laid upon him the punishment of the sins you and I have committed."

I fell in love with Jesus in my teens, not so much for any religious reason that I could identify as because I was an emotional sucker for the self-sacrificing hero. Put a handsome young man in a cart on the way to the gallows, and I was in love. I was devoted to Sidney Carton, sap though I recognized he was; and I'm not sure to this day that I would have liked *Tom Jones* nearly so much if Albert Finney hadn't had his moment of handcuffed nobility before he was carried off on Hugh Griffith's horse to wedded bliss with Susannah York.

So no wonder I fell for Jesus, who willingly went to a torturous death that I read about over and over in Jim Bishop's laboriously detailed *The Day Christ Died.* I must not have been alone, I realize now. That's what Graham is tapping into: the pull of a noble self-sacrifice. His mellifluous baritone voice is throbbing with suppressed emotion. "There is hope for you," he says. "It lies in Christ."

It is a classic pattern, the one he's following; Ignatius of Loyola used it in his spiritual exercises in the sixteenth century. Remind them what God has done for them; remind them of how much they have not done for God; remind them of God's love and desire for them; and then ask them to make a choice.

But it only works if these are reminders, if there is a shared understanding of the way the universe works. It's no wonder the people who come to hear Graham are already believers. If you walked into this stadium not knowing beforehand the story Graham has come to tell, what is going on would make no sense. All you would see would be an old man standing beneath the skull-and-crossbones logo of the Tampa Bay Buccaneers, telling a huge group of admiring listeners that they are worthless scum.

That's what he's talking about now: sin. How truly terrible we are. "The Roman Empire failed because of sin," he says. "There is a right and a wrong, and it's not based on the laws of man but of God. If you break just one of the Ten Commandments you're guilty of breaking all of them. The moment a baby is born, it's a sinner, according to the Bible."

He sounds deeply sorry to be giving us such bad news. "Sin affects our minds," he says. "We want to quit but we can't because we're its slaves. We cry for freedom, but there is no escape. Sin gets on you softly. You don't detect that you're going down, and the more you do the easier it becomes. But there is a penalty. Christ says to the world, you are a sinner, you are going to judgment. Many of you will never know the things God has prepared for those that love him.

"If you never remember anything else," he says now, "remember this one thing, that God loves you." Outside the stadium, Seventh-Day Adventists are handing out a leaflet that addresses the logical conundrum Graham isn't tackling: if God loves us, how come he has consigned so many of us to everlasting torment? Their answer is that he hasn't; the unsaved simply cease to be. The Russian mystic Gurdjieff preached much the same thing: the unenlightened are, in his evocative and terrifying phrase, food for the moon.

But I doubt the Adventists are finding many takers here, because these people know the story. They recognize the scriptural allusions Graham throws into almost every sentence, because they have heard them again and again in sermons and on Christian talk radio. The sin of the world, the narrow road, hope in Christ. These phrases are passwords to a larger understanding of the biblical message that I imagine most of Graham's listeners tonight have rarely questioned: we are sinners from our birth; God's son died to save us from the eternal torment we deserve; and when we die, those who have accepted Christ will go to heaven and everyone else will go to hell.

We think of evangelists as out to change people's beliefs. What Graham is addressing, though, is not belief, but the human experience of loss and complexity. He knows that he is addressing churchgoers, and he knows that religious fervor is a chancy thing. "Many of you tonight feel hopeless," he says. "You feel that your life has been a failure, and you wonder which way to turn. You go to church; you read the Bible once in a while; you pray when you think about it or get in trouble; but does Christ live in your heart?"

And here is the promise. "Paul knew the cross guarantees a future life," he says, quoting Paul's second letter to the Corinthians: "In Christ God was reconciling the world to himself." A woman in the bleachers across the way is yelling, "Amen! Alleluia!" Only inside the story that Graham and his listeners share can Paul's passionate plea for reconciliation be taken as a guarantee of heaven.

"The book of Revelation says we are going to reign with Christ on this earth," he says, then tells the story of a woman who died of starvation when she had a fortune hidden away. "When you think how she wasted away, you think, how foolish. But how much more a fool you would be to hear of God's gift and not accept it."

The solution, he tells us, is simple: Repent, receive Christ into your heart, and obey him. "Do you do that," he asks, "and still don't have total peace? Would you like to leave here *knowing* Jesus lives in you and that you are on the road to heaven? I'm going to ask you to make sure of that. Get up out of your seat right now and stand here."

One of my early experiences of religious confusion came when Graham appeared at a stadium near our house. I was both curious and terrified at the thought of actually going (not that my rigorously skeptical parents would have allowed it). However hard I tried to convince myself Graham was an interesting object of study, in my heart I was convinced that at the altar call, I would leave my seat and come to my knees, sobbing, on the floor of the stadium. How could I not? How could I actually *refuse* God?

But what I'm watching now is nothing like that. If there are tears, I don't see them; it looks like a picnic. People walk down in groups, chatting. There's a man with a camera taking snapshots to bring home with him. Another man stops on the way to tie his little boy's shoelace.

Graham sits on a stool, hunched over. There is a chilly wind, and someone has draped a trenchcoat over his shoulders. The choir is singing softly, "Just as I am, without one plea," and scattered over the stadium floor are signs: Russian; Spanish; German. There were three thousand people down there the night before, Graham told us; it looks like there are going to be at least that many tonight.

He starts to speak softly, almost crooning. "If you're here with friends, come down. They'll wait on you. There's still time to come. Wouldn't it be terrible if one soul was missed? Come, bring a friend or relative with you. There's time. Come not to Billy Graham. Come to the person of Jesus Christ who died for you and rose from the dead and lives forever in heaven. He wants to write your name in the Lamb's book of life. Only those in the book are saved. Are you sure your name is there? It can be."

Read the Bible daily, he says. "You say, but I won't understand it . . . but we're giving you the easiest book in the Bible to take away with you."

I'm expecting it to be the Gospel of Mark, and when he says the book of John, I bat my forehead in sheer bewilderment. John, with his thick helpings of mystical theology, his interminable speeches, his diatribes against the Jews? Even the wonderful stories in John—the woman at the well, the raising of Lazarus, Jesus' washing of his disciples' feet—are hardly simple.

The next day, the Graham organization stages a children's matinee. Graham's not there; his starring role is taken instead by a character named Psalty (short, I assume, for Psalter): a man in a book costume (complete with moving mouth) that covers him from head to hips. Judgment lite. "This is hard to tell," says the book unctuously, "and it might make you sad. Jesus had to die. He took the punishment away.

"Children have incredible faith," the book tells parents in the audience. "They believe anything you tell them, so you have to tell them the right thing." Then he asks any child who wants Jesus to be his forever friend to come down in front of the stage. Huge numbers of kids begin moving. And why not? Who *wouldn't* want a forever friend?

That night, Graham makes his pitch to teenagers. It's youth night, and you can hear the Christian rock from blocks away. Kids are dancing on the stadium floor, and when Graham opens with a joke about the noise level, the audience cheers.

"I have in my hand a Bible," he says, holding it up, "and I'll start in the beginning." But he turns not to the creation of the world, where Genesis actually starts, but to the Fall, two chapters on. "Adam and Eve denied God," he says, "and they were lost, absolutely separated from God, hiding from God." You know what it is to feel lost, he tells the kids, throwing out *ET* and *Saving Private Ryan.*

It's the same message, for an audience that also knows the story, but the tag lines are different. He recites a long list of rock stars who died suddenly. "You never know when your time is coming. I will probably die before you, but you will join me. You have to decide tonight whether you're going to follow Christ or go your own way."

But he also seems to recognize that, to a teenager, heaven seems a long way off. "The men of Galilee were tough and strong and adventurous," he tells them, "and Jesus could take their lives and energy and impulsiveness and use it for God's glory. The Christian faith is for people ready to swim against the tide. Are you?"

When he asks the people on the stadium floor who aren't ready to receive Christ to move back and make room for those who are, all I can think of is Jesus' parable of the separation of the sheep and the goats. But if the reference has also occurred to Graham, he has the good taste to keep it to himself. I am surprised by the number of people who move away; it seems to me that tonight, anyhow, they are the ones who are swimming against the tide, and I admire their courage.

Again, Graham croons the hesitant out of their seats. "The Bible says one soul is worth the whole world. It's worth waiting all night for one person."

A few nights later, I told an old friend, a longtime parish priest, how bewildered I was by all those churchgoers feeling in need of conversion. Or is the altar call more like confession than the once-for-all experience I had imagined it—a quick fix of innocence, until it wears off and you need another?

"You have no idea," he said, "how many people who go to church feel as if they have no relationship with God."

Maybe that's it. The story Graham's hearers share about what the Bible says ties the promise of a relationship with God to another promise—one that can't really be kept. Accept Christ, it says, and you will *know*, know for certain, that all will be well with you forever.

Early Christian converts knew better; they would delay baptism until their deathbed because they recognized that—once baptized, cleansed of sin, and saved—they would, if given the chance, sin again. If, as the early church taught, confession as well as baptism was a once-in-a-lifetime event, to confess your sins while you still had a lifetime to commit more was to recklessly court damnation.

It all depends on how you read the story.

II. SOCIETY OF
BIBLICAL LITERATURE CONVENTION

San Francisco, CA

Hanging around at Kennedy Airport waiting for the plane to San Francisco, I gradually realize that most of my fellow passengers are bound for the same event: the annual meeting of the American Academy of Religion and the Society for Biblical Literature. Whole divinity schools close down for this weekend, I am told by a group from Princeton. The hundreds of presentations on offer fill all the meeting rooms of three hotels. Wandering down the maze of corridors, it's easy to forget not only which floor you're on, but which hotel you're in.

If you are professionally involved in the teaching of religion—and even more if you are *hoping* to be involved in the teaching of religion—this is the place to be.

I am approaching this weekend with a bit of a chip on my shoulder. Back home, in my parish Bible study, we have been looking at the hypothetical Gospel source known as *Q*, and the claims of some *Q* scholars have made my hackles rise. The theory itself makes sense; it's based on scholars' observation that while much of Luke and Matthew seem to be based on Mark, the two also share material that isn't in Mark. Presumably that material comes from another source. German scholars extracted those passages and called the resultant document *Q*, the first letter of the German word for source.

But give a biblical scholar a hypothesis, and before you know it you've got a community, a history, and a theology. In particular, I am irritated by *Q* scholars' insistence that their "*Q* community" wasn't interested in the crucifixion. After all, I figure, *Q* is, by definition, the material Luke and Matthew share that isn't in Mark. But when something is in all three of them, as the crucifixion is, how can you know whether it was in *Q* or not?

The first evening, I meet Marcus Borg—not a *Q* specialist but, as a Jesus scholar, familiar with the debate—at a lobby bar. There are ways, he tells me. For one thing, he says, if there was anything in *Q* about the crucifixion, you would expect to find Matthew and Luke sharing details that aren't in Mark, and they don't. I am not convinced. I suspect I don't want to be. The crucifixion is important to me; I want it to be important to *Q*, too.

Q is the focus of a swirl of academic politics, Borg adds, clueing me in on the panels to watch. What you think about *Q* says a lot about how you think Christianity developed, he says, and that's a hot topic these days.

But over the weekend I come to realize that, though early Christianity is getting a lot of media attention—with Jesus on the cover of all three newsweeklies, and a PBS special on the early church—the center of academic attention has shifted. The *really* hot topic at the SBL is what is broadly termed reader-response criticism. The approach, which originated in literature departments, is based on the theory that the meaning of a piece of writing (a "text" in academese) is determined by the reader, not the writer. Instead of trying to find the "truth" of biblical accounts, these scholars look at how readers interpret them.

I have barely begun to grasp the concept when I go to hear "The Implications of Gender-Bending in Micah." Since the paper is based on a complex interpretation of apparent corruptions in the ancient Hebrew text, I am a bit over my depth. But in fact the thesis isn't hard to grasp. What had always been seen as corruptions in the text, the speaker argues, are in fact deliberate attempts to shake up the reader's perceptions of gender. The book, she proclaims, consists of three acts in drag, in which the characters are brutally punished for gender transgressions.

She makes (as far as I, with no knowledge of Hebrew, can tell) an interesting and, in its own terms, persuasive case. Assume Jerusalem, Samaria, and Zion to be characters, not geographical areas; and take the subject of the book to be sexual roles and their consequences, not purity of worship and social justice, and you can bend genders into pretzels.

"Recognizing gender codes in biblical texts is tricky," she says early on in what I can only take to be an understatement. "I have had to find my own."

And so she does. Yahweh shepherding his flock with a staff is an image of the thrusting male; cutting off Samaria's idols is stripping her of signs of male power; Jerusalem will be punished for her assertiveness by being plowed like a field ("in other words, fucked"); and Zion is armed by a male Yahweh with male tools (including a horn of iron, "a terrifying phallic symbol") for male activity.

"The text," she tells us, "plays the audience. Genderfuck, if we take the term seriously, opens a space of self-referentiality, and produces alienation. The violence of the response plays a role in pushing the reader to evaluate and challenge the ideological framework that demands such a sadistic response."

I wonder just what reader she has in mind. Gender-bending was not, as far as I know, a concept familiar to the Hebrews of the seventh century B.C.E.; and modern readers, who might have some grasp of the concept, are not generally fluent in ancient Hebrew. Just who is she talking about?

Herself, it seems; the proof she cites for her argument is that that's how the text has affected her. The text has made her change her behavior; her changed behavior validates her theory. She gets a lot of applause.

The Micah paper is preceded by a dual presentation from a man in a sports jacket and ponytail and a woman in black with unkempt hair. They hand a paper back and forth, reading it in turns, and then begin to act it out. The woman gestures wildly, then hands the man a card that he first refuses and then takes. When the paper (or performance, I'm not sure which) is over, she takes off her gloves. There are no questions.

I am curious about a paper on the drunkenness of Noah; on a trip to Florence I'd discovered that the story, which I barely knew, was a favorite of Renaissance artists and sculptors.

It's an odd tale: After the flood, Noah gets drunk in his tent. His son Ham comes in, sees him naked, and runs out. His other sons Shem and Japheth then back into the tent and, taking care not to look, cover their father up. When he wakes, Noah curses Ham—a curse picked up centuries later to justify slavery.

If Ham's offense was really only the innocent oversight it is described to be, Noah's curse seems a dramatic overreaction. Any Freudian would start asking pointed questions. Nor did ancient readers miss the sexual undercurrents of the story; in the

Talmud, two prominent third-century rabbis argued over whether Ham raped his father or castrated him.

This speaker gets even more creative. Noah was the aggressor, she says; he took off his clothes *after* Ham entered the tent, raped him, then cursed him out of his own sense of guilt. Perhaps Noah was a henpecked husband, doubting his masculinity, she suggests. In that case, his curse of Ham would be a symbolic castration.

I can't figure out whether this is a game of which I don't know the rules, or a serious stab at Freudian interpretation. But didn't Freud, when he interpreted myths, stick to the plot? Doesn't even the possibility of mutual discourse go out the window, if each reader is free to rewrite the story before responding to it?

A man in the audience asks if she thinks this is the way it really happened. "In the mind of the storyteller," he says, "Noah was not the initiator."

"You never know what's in the writer's mind," she responds, casually dismissing his question.

I don't know what to make of this; I have spent years in Bible studies in which the first issue addressed was what's in the writer's mind.

But I am developing a theory about the dynamics of academic life. The halls here are jammed with newly minted Ph.D.s desperately seeking tenure-track positions in biblical studies. Their sheer numbers, I figure, go a long way towards explaining the quirkiness of so many of the theories I'm hearing expounded. After all, to get a Ph.D., you have to do original research. After a few thousand years, and millions of volumes, of biblical studies, finding something original to say must take a lot of imagination.

In a session on biblical lament in the age of AIDS, I get introduced to queer theory—which, from what the speaker says, is not so much about sex as it is about culture. "Queer" stands for whatever is at odds with the dominant culture.

Listening to this speaker is, for me, like trying to figure out Paul's letters to the Corinthians. Like Paul, he's arguing with people whose position I can only deduce by what he says about them. His opponents seem to be insisting that the Bible, and in particular the Psalms, should not be read by people with AIDS. They are dangerous, the argument seems to go, because they teach submission to suffering, something people with AIDS should be resisting.

But the speaker, clearly feeling himself on controversial ground, argues that it's a good and helpful thing for readers to engage with texts "in which suffering is vocalized by the person who is suffering." Reading texts in which the speaker confronts God increases readers' radicalism, he says. "It gives readers a precedent for recognizing the tragic dimension of their situation."

He also approves of reading psalms of praise, because he says they offer a recognition of the importance of hope. But he warns against reading psalms of repentance—they could, he says, lead readers to blame themselves.

Here is a still different reader: not the controller of the text, but its victim. This speaker, and his opponents, both seem to assume that the reader is merely a passive absorber of whatever passes in front of his eyes. In this interpretation, texts are dangerous objects. Without a guide to choose and interpret them, they will lead readers astray.

He ends his paper with a call for safer texts and safer readings.

After the session, I tell him that I belong to a church in Greenwich Village that has been dealing with AIDS since its first appearance. Never, I say, would it have occurred to us not to use the Psalms, which we don't merely read, but pray. I get the verbal equivalent of a pat on the back. "I'm glad to know," he says, "that what I am suggesting in theory is being put into practice."

"I think," I respond, "it's happening more than you know."

Later I run into an old friend—one of those newly minted Ph.D.s, who had been on the staff of my parish when we were being decimated by AIDS—and tell her about the session. "The discontinuity between academia and what's happening in the churches," she says, "is astonishing."

Reader-response criticism may be the hot topic in biblical academia, but since it hasn't reached the mainstream, it's not where the stars are. Academics are no less impressed than the rest of us by fame and fortune. And the people getting the magazine covers and TV shows and best-seller accolades are Jesus scholars. Half-a-dozen books on Jesus have come out in the past few years, and to the astonishment of the media, they've sold well. On his lecture tours, Marcus Borg admits, in some embarrassment, to making a very good living talking about a Jesus who had a preference for the poor.

Jesus studies are also where competitiveness runs most rampant. The standard format at this affair is for one scholar to present a paper, on which a panel then comments. In the Jesus sessions, once the paper is finished, the knives—on both sides—come out. One speaker attacks his critic's anthropological sources and credentials. "I don't see how you could have missed this if you were trained in anthropology."

Another panel gets into a wrangle over a psychological analysis that lays great stress on Jesus' being the first-born in his family. "How can you say that Jesus had a positive relationship with Joseph just because he used God-father language?" asks Borg. "Why not say he used it because he didn't have one and wanted it—like me?" The speaker is raked over the coals for using a developmental model on data much too sparse and uncertain to carry it; for trying to make too much of the little data he does have; for assuming that a twentieth-century psychological model makes sense when applied to a first-century Jewish peasant. The only thing they like about his paper is the appendix.

One refreshingly frank speaker owns up to the search for uniqueness that underlies a lot of this. "I could describe my Jesus this way," he says blithely, "but then I couldn't distinguish him from Crossan's Jesus."

I am startled, as I am every time I run into the Jesus scholars, at how very little of the Gospels they are willing to accept as factual. "No, I don't think the resurrection was divine intervention," says one. Another suggests that the assembled panel reach agreement on a statement that Jesus did not rise. "I assume there isn't a real Holy Spirit out there in the world," says another, "but if there was, my conclusion would be about the same."

And theology is a dirty word. "I'm trying to give an explanation of what caused people to have faith that's not a theological answer," says one speaker. "I don't think it was divine intervention." Another speaker stumbles over the phrase "theory of ideology," then jokes, "I almost said theology."

Their assumption that God is irrelevant to the study of the Bible makes me edgy. I feel like the butt of some media-fed joke about evangelists and snake handlers, as though my religious faith automatically disqualifies me for serious intellectual discussion. It isn't fair, I know; some of the best-known Jesus scholars—Borg among them—are deeply religious. But here in their hive, the easy cynicism takes over.

The panels featuring big stars like Marcus Borg, John Dominic Crossan, and Raymond Brown have been jammed, forcing me to watch from such a distance that I'm not always sure exactly who's speaking. But I arrive early to get a front seat for the biggest celebrity of all, the only person here, as far as I know, who's won a Pulitzer Prize. The SBL has joined up with *Publishers Weekly* to bring Jack Miles, author of *God: A Biography,* to San Francisco to talk about writing for a popular audience.

If I needed anything to confirm my suspicion that a lot of the people here don't care about writing for a popular audience, this session produces it. The auditorium is no more than respectably full. Miles, who has spent much of his career as a journalist, is not a member of the club—a fact of which he is obviously acutely aware. Instead of coaching academics on the tricks of bestsellerdom, he attacks them, championing the role of public intellectual in which he sees himself.

It's a role academia has noticed, but not embraced. A recent University of Chicago conference, he tells us, included a panel discussion entitled "The Public Intellectual—Threat or Menace?" "The disjunction escapes me," he says dryly, "but the language bespeaks both anxiety and confusion."

Stop thinking about your own career for a minute, he tells them, and think about your audience. "The American public would be better off if the knowledge produced in it were more widely shared. And knowledge of the Bible is one category every knowledge worker should have. But you must recognize you are writing for readers just as intellectual, just as trained as you are, but differently. To reach them, you have to force yourself to go where *you* are a beginner."

Miles is speaking not to the academic elite, but to the masses: the teaching assistants and part-time faculty desperate for a tenure-track job they have little hope of getting. You're better off without one, he says. Yes, it's hard to fit scholarship into the harried schedule of an ordinary salaried American, he says, but it can be done: "The intellectual life and the academic life have never coincided to the extent they do here."

And you will be free, he says, free to delve into whatever interests you, to read for your own pleasure and excitement, to explore broadly, maybe even to produce a work powerful enough to transform the culture. "I could not have written *God,*" he says, "if I had not been away from academe for many years."

At the end of the day, I drop in at one of the dozens of receptions that almost eliminate the need for real meals. I am playing the conference game of scanning name tags, looking for someone worth talking to, when I spot a middle-aged man wearing a plaid shirt and an I-know-something-you-don't smile, talking to another man who's looking a bit nervous. The smiler is wearing a label describing him as a representative of the Society for Prophecy Reformation.

"What is that?" I ask, strolling over.

"He'll tell you," says his current victim, making a dash for the bar. Too late, I realize that I have fallen into the hands of a True Nut. The prophecies of Jesus, he tells me, have already been fulfilled, if only we could see it.

"Paul didn't think so," I say.

He nods sagely. "He was right. It happened later."

"When?"

"When and how Jesus said it would."

This is not getting anywhere, and I'm not sure I want it to. In a stab at changing the subject, I ask him what he's doing here. "It must not be a very fertile field." He gives me that knowing smile again, and I flee back to the roast beef. But he follows me.

"Can I ask a question? What did you mean by saying it wasn't a fertile field?"

I explain that as far as I can tell, only about 20 percent of the people here believe the Bible contains even the smallest nuggets of fact. They're hardly likely to worry about whether Jesus' prophecies have come true.

He looks at me, bewildered. "But if they don't believe the Bible is true," he asks finally, "why do they spend time studying it?"

"Good question," I say. "I've been tempted to ask it myself."

"They don't think it's true?"

I correct myself. "No, that's not fair. They don't think it's factual. Some of them do think it contains stories with deep truths."

"But why do they study it if it's no different from any other story?"

"Well, for one thing," I say, "it's how they make a living."

"They do this for a living? All these people?"

"Yes," I say. "You've walked into a nest of professional biblical scholars."

Light dawns. "Oh," he says. "Well, thank you for taking the time."

He walks out the door.

III. MARBLE COLLEGIATE CHURCH

New York City

The usher at Marble Collegiate Church, an elderly black man with calloused hands, greets me as though he's determined to prove, singlehandedly, that New Yorkers can be friendly. He shakes my hand when I walk in; he leads me to a pew; and when he tells me how glad he is to see me here today, I believe him. The board of ushers and greeters at Marble has over forty members, and from what I can tell, at least half of them are at work this morning. No stray visitors are going to slip unnoticed into the pews here.

Marble Collegiate bills itself as America's hometown church. Its claim to that title is perhaps not as self-evident now as it was in the 1950s, when Congress voted to put "IN GOD WE TRUST" on our coins, and Marble's former pastor, Norman Vincent Peale, ruled the Sunday morning airwaves, an icon of American Christianity.

But for all its size, its vaulted ceiling and its dusty red grandeur, there is indeed something homey about Marble. For me, and I suspect for almost everyone over a certain age who walks through its doors, this is what church used to be. There's an American flag in the corner. The people filling the pews are dressed with a kind of everyday formality, neither snobbish nor disrespectful. Most of the women are wearing skirts, and most of the men, jackets. The three chairs on the platform in front of us are banked with greenery, and the organ is quietly noodling away at an Aaron Copland piece. Everyone looks glad to be here.

Marble has changed with the times. Its congregation now contains many young professionals, so listed in today's program is a Career Empowerment session on the secrets of a successful job interview, as well as a Women's Forum dinner meeting featuring Phyllis Tribble, a prominent feminist interpreter of the Bible. The church's staff of two dozen includes a resident Bible scholar—a Roman Catholic nun.

In American religious mythology, though, Marble will forever be the home of the idealized American Christianity of the '50s: welcoming, accepting, unfrightening—a place for good people to gather every week to give an hour to God in the hope that he will, in return, enrich their lives. "The Marble vision is a vibrant one that seeks always a deeper insight and a higher ground," said one of the pieces of literature I picked up in the lobby. "People's lives are changed at Marble."

I had come to Marble, on the Sunday after the Littleton, Colorado, shootings, to see what I could see about the role of the Bible in the mythic American religion it represents.

"We are in sacred space," intones Arthur Caliandro, the church's senior minister, opening the service. "Worship God."

"As we begin the service, we ask for a fresh touch of your spirit," prays the only woman among the three ministers leading the service. "Let the light of thy presence shine on our hearts and minds that we may receive thy word to us this day."

The word in question this week is Psalm 46, with its well-known urging to "be still and know that I am God." Listen to these words, Caliandro urges us—but he's not talking about the reading. He's talking about the hymn, "Drop Thy Still Dews of Quietness," that follows it.

Though today's theme is quietness, the service is anything but, including as it does, not one sermon but two, the other titled "A Layperson Speaks." Three, actually, counting the lengthy ruminations about the Littleton tragedy that precede Caliandro's pastoral prayer. We have lost our sense of compassion, he says; we have allowed our dark side to run amok. "We are too immature as a people to have violent weapons."

He talks about Mothers Against Violence. "Fifteen years ago, no one would have thought we could turn the tide against smoking. Maybe while we are still alive, violence will be unpopular to the American people." He asks us to pray for the parents who have lost their children and for the soul of America.

After a hymn (a de-gendered version of "Dear Lord and Father of Mankind, Forgive Our Foolish Ways"), Caliandro introduces today's featured layperson, who's going to talk about what church membership means to her. The church's new-member sessions begin next week, and this is the first of two pitches to join up; Caliandro makes another later in the service.

"Marble is an oasis of warm, loving, kind, generous people," says the tall black woman, a former church employee who's now in law school. "When I joined, there were no demands made, but there were a lot of needs met. The challenges I faced on a daily basis became a lot easier to handle."

If you join, she says, "you are certain to gain many privileges. And I will go one step further. They will be delivered with love, unwavering support, and unconditional acceptance."

"That's the best legal brief I've heard in a long time," says

Caliandro enthusiastically, putting his arm around her. "I don't know how anybody can make it in New York without help."

Neither of them has mentioned God.

At the announcements, Caliandro reads off the distant places from which visitors have come today. I'm impressed that the ushers have managed to gather that information and get it to Caliandro so quickly. They're an efficient bunch. They're also well choreographed; as they collect the offering, they move in unison from pew to pew. It's the most ceremonial part of the service.

Caliandro starts his sermon by talking about how difficult it is for all of us to sit alone in a room and be quiet. "We live in an incredibly noisy world," he says, citing everything from vacuum cleaners to snowmobiles to loud music at wedding receptions. How to address the problem? A church member has a suggestion, he says. Through the League for the Hard of Hearing, he has established Noise Awareness Day, and he'll have a table at coffee hour.

It is hard to avoid the suspicion that Noise Awareness Day came first, and the need to be still and know that God is God, second. But Caliandro does finally turn to the day's reading. "We need to look to the wisdom of the ages, much of which is found in the Holy Bible. It's so wise. It talks about noise and silence. It mentions the tumult, the noise, the disturbance, the conflict, the tension, the rumble we live in . . . and yet God is in the midst of it. The climactic verse—verse 10—'Be still'"—he pauses dramatically—"'and know that I am God.' Wherever you are on your spiritual journey, I have a sense you know what I'm talking about. In stillness, and maybe only in stillness, can we experience the depth and breadth and power of God."

He turns to Psalm 23. "Imagine yourself lying on the grass, with the birds flying overhead and the rustle of the wind. He leads me beside still waters, and what does that do? It restores my soul."

Jesus, too, in crisis, went to stillness, he says. "He sought out a quiet and lonely place. He went to the Garden of Gethsemane and there, in its beauty and stillness, he fought the battle of life. And in the beginning of his ministry, when he was tempted, he went to the mountain for forty days alone in the quiet. He battled in the quiet and in the quiet found victory. When he was on the sea and in the storm, his words were 'Peace, be still.'" Caliandro is reaching for it, I think. Quietness is not the main feature of any of those stories.

And what do we do? Caliandro asks. We turn up the volume and run away from ourselves. The sermon ends, as I suspect many of Caliandro's sermons do, with some practical suggestions: Strive for a quiet heart, and set aside quiet holy time. "Lord, help us in this noisy world to find a quiet heart," he prays, "and the peace which passeth all understanding."

I leave the church wondering, somewhat to my surprise, just what they are afraid of. They are protesting too much: telling us too often, and too loudly, of our welcome and our acceptance—acceptance not by God so much as by the Marble community. Caliandro urged his listeners to turn to the Bible as though he was quite certain it was something they would never, naturally, think of doing, and I imagine he's right.

Lurking under the surface of the warm welcome at Marble, it seemed to me, was a vision not of an accepting God, but of one who demands, judges, and rejects; and of a Bible that is the record of that God's rules and of his wrath. It's a common enough vision of God. In a Bible study at a Jesuit center on Wall Street, I met a woman who proudly showed me a picture of a saint of whom I had never heard. Her parish priest had handed them out wholesale, instructing his parishioners to mount them on their bedroom walls. There, he told them, "it will protect you from the wrath of God."

"What are they teaching them in these churches?" I exploded to the Jesuit who ran the center. He shrugged in embarrassment.

But distorted as it is, that vision of a wrathful God arises, at least in part, out of a profound recognition that terror is part of our experience of the Holy. Marble seemed to me to be offering itself not as a way into that experience, but as a way around it: a safe, welcoming, blandly affable substitute.

IV. READING THE BIBLE

Are these people all talking about the same book?

The short answer, of course, is yes. They are all talking about the collection of sacred writings that was pulled together by the early Christian church. A thousand years later, the invention of printing allowed those writings to be bound together in a single volume, labeled the Bible, or the Scriptures, or—its most loaded title by far—the Word of God.

In fact, though, the Bible is an anthology, not a book. The works it contains were written over more than a thousand years, in three languages, by writers of many different cultures.

What's more, unlike most anthologies—which, once they're put together, stay that way—the Bible has been a shifting target. Some of its contents circulated for centuries before being written down; once written, they were copied, rewritten, combined, and rewritten again by countless hands before anyone ever thought of gathering them into a single collection.

It wasn't until the fourth century C.E. that the Bible became the collection of books we now know; and even today, there is not one Bible, but three. Although most Christians would equate their Old Testament with the Hebrew scriptures, the two are not the same. Jews call their sacred book the *Tanakh* (an acronym for the Hebrew names of its three sections); though it contains most of the same material as the Christian Old Testament, the order is very different.

Nor do Christians agree among themselves about what goes into the Bible. Roman Catholic Bibles contain a chunk of late pre-Christian material known as the Apocrypha. Most Protestant Bibles leave it out.

For American readers (indeed, for all readers except those who know ancient Hebrew, Greek, and Aramaic) the confusion is compounded by the translation issue. There is no standard translation of the Bible; new ones are published every year or so.

One of the classic ones—the sixteenth-century King James version—is not only still around but regarded by many Americans as the only acceptable translation, either for theological reasons or because of its extraordinary poetic beauty. (Some of its enthusiasts, in what may or may not be a slip of the tongue, describe it as the *Saint* James version.)

Translation is a difficult art at best; translation of ancient documents, whose text may be so corrupt and confusing as to force the translator to guess at the meaning, is even more complicated. When the documents in question are regarded by millions of readers as the Word of God, the project carries an almost unbearable weight. Whole doctrines can hang on the change of a single word.

Take, for instance, the Virgin Birth—the Christian doctrine that Mary, having been impregnated not naturally by Joseph, but supernaturally by the Holy Spirit, was still a virgin when she gave birth to Jesus. Matthew's Gospel uses a well-known verse in the book of Isaiah to support that assertion. In the King James version, it's translated "Behold, a virgin shall conceive and bear a son."

But in the original Hebrew, the word that the KJV renders as "virgin" is *almah*, which simply means young woman. What Matthew was quoting, and the text the KJV translators were relying on, wasn't a Hebrew text. It was a Greek translation, the Septuagint, produced in the fourth century B.C.E. And the Septuagint translates *almah* with the Greek word *parthenos*, which does mean "virgin." From such linguistic threads hang great swaths of doctrine.

Translators also struggle with the question—not easily answered—of just what it means to be faithful to the original text. Phrases that meant one thing in the ancient world can mean quite another—or nothing at all—today. And that's assuming that we even know what they meant to the ancient writer, which in many cases we don't. Where should a translator's loyalty lie? To the words themselves, even if a modern reader is likely to misunderstand some of them? Or to the thoughts behind the words?

Most of the best-known modern translations, like the Revised Standard Version and the New International Version, are straightforward attempts to reproduce in English, as accurately

as possible, the words of the original text. They leave the interpretation of that text up to the reader, or at least limit their interpretive efforts to the notes and commentary.

But many translations, particularly from the more doctrinaire
ends of the Christian tradition, try to translate the writer's thoughts
into language that will be clear to a contemporary reader. Some of
these paraphrases are more tendentious than others, but they
share a desire to make sure the reader gets the right message,
whether that message is feminist or fundamentalist.

Here, for instance, is a passage from the letter to the Ephesians as it appears in the New Revised Standard Version:

> God put this power to work in Christ when he raised him
> from the dead and seated him at his right hand in the heav-
> enly places, far above all rule and authority and power and
> dominion, and above every name that is named, not only in
> this age but also in the age to come. And he has put all
> things under his feet and has made him the head over all
> things for the church, which is his body, the fullness of him
> who fills all in all.

And here's how that passage appears in *The Message*, a recent
and popular paraphrase by Eugene Peterson:

> All this energy issues from Christ: God raised him from
> death and set him on a throne in deep heaven, in charge of
> running the universe, everything from galaxies to govern-
> ments, no name and no power exempt from his rule. And
> not just for the time being, but *forever*. He is in charge of
> it all, has the final word on everything. At the center of all
> this, Christ rules the church. The church, you see, is not
> peripheral to the world; the world is peripheral to the
> church. The church is Christ's body, in which he speaks and
> acts, by which he fills everything with his presence.

Left-wing translators take similar liberties; an inclusive-
language lectionary produced a few years ago gets rid not only of
masculine references to God, but just about anything else that

could conceivably offend any imaginable interest group (except, of course, conservatives). Among its excisions: references to "the right hand of God," a common phrase in both the Old Testament and the New. When I asked one of the translators involved in the lectionary how she could call that a translation, she defended it vigorously. "Some of those decisions are in fact legitimate translations," she argued, "because we are dealing with metaphors that had particular meanings in their contexts of origin, but that weren't literal descriptions. I think it's important, where the metaphor has a hurtful consequence, to spend time probing to the meaning behind the metaphor, which is what we were attempting to do."

Complex and tendentious as they are, none of these issues fully accounts for the staggering interpretive gap between Billy Graham and—to take a comparatively mild example—the SBL participant who simply rules out divine inspiration as a possible factor in the early church's explosive growth. Their argument is not over the words on the page, but where those words came from. For most scholars, the Bible, like any other book, is a completely human document. Its sacredness, if they believe it has any, comes only from the community that has regarded it as sacred. Its inspiration comes only from the hearts of its diverse group of writers and the various cultures they inhabited. In analyzing it, then, any scholarly technique is legitimate.

For Billy Graham, the Bible is a divine document, inspired, if not actually dictated, by God, and containing God's message to humanity. It has a single subject, salvation, and a single protagonist, Jesus Christ, through whom that salvation has come. To view the Bible through any other lens is to court damnation.

Modern American Christians, even those who disagree with it, generally see Graham's reading as the normative one. That, they believe, is how Christians have read the Bible through the centuries, unchallenged until the rise of modern biblical scholarship in the nineteenth century. Like Billy Graham, most American Christians assume the Bible was intended to be, and has always been understood to be, a book about facts. If the facts are wrong, so is the Bible.

That's the view underlying the crusade of Episcopal bishop John Spong to demolish what he describes as the traditional Christian understanding of God. "Only one thing will save this venerable faith tradition at this critical time in Christian history," Spong declared in a message posted on the Internet, "and that is a new Reformation far more radical than Christianity has ever before known [which] must deal with the very substance of that faith."

Put briefly, Spong's argument is that since a literal reading of the Bible is scientific nonsense, doctrines based on the Bible need to be trashed. "The biblical story of the perfect and finished creation from which human beings fell into sin is pre-Darwinian mythology and post-Darwinian nonsense," he said in thesis 3 (of 12).

Both Spong and Graham go to the Bible seeking "just the facts, ma'am." Graham thinks he's getting them; Spong is sure he isn't. But their assumptions are identical. Along with most biblical scholars and indeed most American Christians, they are stuck in what Marcus Borg, who as a Jesus scholar has perpetrated some himself, calls "fact fundamentalism."

"I think we live, we modern Westerners, in the only culture that has ever identified truth so tightly with factuality," he told me in one conversation. "Our almost knee-jerk reaction is that if it isn't scientifically verifiable, or if it's not a historically reliable fact, it's not true."

"Well, of course," a modern Bible reader would say. Before Darwin, who could have doubted Genesis? Before the development of medical science, what reason was there to question Jesus' miracles?

The truth, though, is that since there was a Bible, its most faithful readers have challenged, questioned, and poked holes in it. It didn't take a Clarence Darrow to point out the illogic of God's creating light on the first day, and the sun on the fourth, in the first Genesis creation story; St. Augustine made the same point in the fourth century. Origen, in the third century, observed tartly that there is no mountain high enough to let the Devil show Jesus all the kingdoms of the earth, and scoffed at the notion of God physically strolling around the Garden of Eden. John Chrysostom, in the fourth century, accused Paul of "misuse of language."

Some of the most searching and imaginative biblical readers were the rabbis of the first few centuries C.E., for whom the contradictions and gaps of scripture offered, as one scholar puts it, the pieces of grit around which they could construct the pearls of midrash. Their puzzlement over how Abraham, living in a pagan culture, became a monotheist and follower of God produced multiple explanations: he learned it hiding alone in a cave; he deduced it logically; in perhaps the most ingenious explanation, he learned it from his kidneys. "Abraham's father did not teach him," said a second-century rabbi. "Nor did Abraham have a rabbi. How did he learn this essential teaching of Torah? God appointed his two kidneys to be two teachers and they taught him wisdom. This is why it is written in Scripture, *I bless the Lord who gives me counsel; in the night my kidneys instruct me.*"

They saw, as acutely as any modern reader, the moral intricacy and ambivalence of many biblical stories. Why did God test Abraham by demanding that he sacrifice his son Isaac? In one rabbinic account, it sprang from Isaac's chutzpah. In this version, Isaac is not a child, but an adult, and one day he gets into an argument with his older half-brother Ishmael over which of them is more worthy to be Abraham's heir. "I am," argues Ishmael. "I was thirteen when I was circumcised, and I allowed it to happen. You were only eight days old. If you could have prevented it, maybe you would have."

"But I am an adult now," responds Isaac. "If God asks for all my limbs, I would not refuse." It was after this conversation, the rabbi says, that God tested Abraham.

A sixth-century poet gave Sarah, Abraham's wife, the passionate voice that, in this story, the book of Genesis denies her. "If he who first gave the child wants it back, why did he offer him at all," she asks Abraham indignantly. "Do you, old man, leave what is mine with me . . . I will not entrust the child to you."

Its ancient readers searched the Bible not nearly so much for facts as for meaning. And not just one meaning, but layer after layer. In the Middle Ages, scholars held that every text had four—or in some views as many as seven—different senses. The four primary ones—literal, allegorical, moral, and anagogical— were summed up in a catchy rhyme:

> The letter shows us what God and our fathers did;
> The allegory shows us where our faith is hid;
> The moral meaning gives us rules of daily life;
> The anagogy shows us where we end our strife.

Even Thomas Aquinas, who argued against the tendency to allegorize scripture, acknowledged its multiple meanings. "It is not unfitting," he wrote in the *Summa Theologica,* "if even according to the literal sense one word in holy scripture should have several senses."

The difference between these ancient readers and us is not that they were blind to the Bible's contradictions and complexity. It's that these characteristics did not, for them, threaten its sacredness. Instead, they seem to have confirmed it. Only God, you can almost hear them saying, could bring meaning and order out of such apparent chaos.

They did not agree, any more than we do, on what that meaning was. "The debate between the Dominicans and the Franciscans in the Middle Ages over whether Jesus' disciples owned possessions make our current controversies look trivial," Stanley Hauerwas told me in a telephone conversation. "But their arguments were about what the Bible was about. Our arguments now are about what the Bible is, since we don't think it tells us about the way things are."

The rise of rationalism in the eighteenth century destroyed that consensus. All of a sudden, the Bible was being asked questions that its writers had never dreamed of answering. As the scientific viewpoint became more and more the measure of all things, biblical contradictions that had left the ancients unfazed became huge stumbling blocks. "In a divine book everything is true," wrote Ernest Renan in the nineteenth century of the

reasoning that drove him out of the church. "And since two contradictory statements cannot be true at the same time, there
must be no contradictions in it. Now the attentive study that I
made of the Bible, while revealing historical and aesthetic treas-
ures to me, also proved to me that this book was no more exempt
than any other ancient book from contradictions, mistakes,
errors."

Scholars began treating the Bible as they did other ancient
books, trying to separate myth from fact. H. S. Reimarus argued
in the eighteenth century that the historical Jesus had been a
failed Jewish revolutionary, and that the Christ of the church was
invented by the disciples, who stole the body from the tomb.

Nineteenth-century scholars began picking apart the strands
out of which the Bible was created. They discovered that the
Torah, or first five books of the Old Testament, did not have a
single author (and was *certainly* not written by Moses). Instead
it was a melding of northern and southern epics (called *E* and *J*
for the first letters of the words each uses for God) which were
then revised, with additions (known as *P*), by a member of the
priestly class; and finally topped off with the addition of the book
of Deuteronomy (*D*), which actually stems from the historical
books that follow the Torah.

New Testament scholars, meanwhile, were arguing that the
Gospel of Mark was not, as Augustine had thought, a shortened
version of Matthew, but instead a source not only for Matthew
but for Luke as well. To fill in the gaps, they deduced the existence of still another source, never discovered in written form,
which they called *Q*. And the quest for the historical Jesus, which
began in the eighteenth century, hasn't ended yet, in spite of
attempts by everyone from Albert Schweitzer to Luke Timothy
Johnson to stop it in its tracks.

All of this historical and linguistic excavation has been invalu-
able in helping us understand the cultures out of which the Bible
comes, the development of its theologies, and the beliefs and
intentions of those who contributed to its creation. But it also
went a long way toward destroying, at least for the world of scholars and those who listened to them, any conviction that the Bible

tells a story worth hearing. The Bible became a text to be mastered; the ancient concept of the Bible as revelation, as something that reads us even as we read it, no longer seemed to make sense.

In a culture that had completely accepted the rationalist viewpoint—that fact equals truth—this view of the Bible shook Christianity to its core. If you accepted it, the Bible either lost all meaning or became spiritualized and irrelevant. If you defied it—and many did—you defied the basic assumptions of your culture. Fundamentalism sprang out of that defiance—a last-ditch, digging-in-the-heels insistence that the Bible *was so* true. But even fundamentalism is a creature of rationalism; witness its twisted use of scientific method, in so-called scientific creationism, to "prove" the Bible's absolute facticity.

I am not arguing that we should return to those ancient readings. For one thing, we can't. We are the children of rationalism. We know what we know, and, unless we turn fundamentalist, cannot un-know it. The Bible is our Humpty Dumpty. It has fallen off its pedestal and broken into pieces, and we are left standing around wondering how we will ever manage to put it together again.

This book started as an investigation into what Americans mean when they say they read the Bible. What book do they think they are reading? What is its purpose? What do they want and expect from it?

But as I traveled around the country listening to people talk about the Bible, and thinking about what they said, I started asking a new question: Is there a way of reading the Bible that recognizes all that we have learned about it—its many strands, its complex history, the human intricacies of its development—and allows it, in and through all of that, to be a place of encounter with God?

Chapter 2

First Congregational Church

Colorado Springs, CO

I t's not easy to be a liberal in Colorado Springs, home of the Christian Right. Ask Jim White, pastor of the First Congregational Church. His church's bitter battle over the blessing of gay unions culminated in White's being sent for "psychiatric evaluation" by denominational officials. (He returned to his church in triumph after his congregation's sizeable psychiatric population rallied to his support, protesting against a misuse of their profession.)

When Bill Moyers went to Colorado Springs to make a documentary about the battle there over gay rights, he used White, his church, and a lesbian couple whose union White blessed, as a centerpiece. "I got my ten minutes of fame," White grins. "I said the coach of the University of Colorado football team quotes Leviticus that it is an abomination in the eyes of the Lord for a man to lie with a man. But if he reads further, he will come to where it says it's an abomination to touch the skin of a dead pig. And there goes football."

White's biblical literacy is not shared by most of his congregation—or indeed by most in the United Church of Christ, the denomination to which First Congregational belongs. In an attempt to find out why not, and what can be done about it, the denomination has begun studying the place of scripture in its churches. Its Scripture Project put together six studies on passages throughout the Bible that in some way address the role of scripture. Each study is designed to get participants talking about how they feel about, and use, the Bible. White was leading some of those studies while I was there.

It's a mixed dozen that gathers around folding tables in the church library, everyone from teenagers to retirees. The lesson tonight is what may be the Christian church's earliest creedal statement, from Paul's letter to the Philippians. White, an enthusiastic, jokey man who runs the constant risk of seeming flip, has each person read a portion. They're using a wild hodgepodge of translations, everything from the KJV to *The Message*.

White barrages the group with questions. What are the positive words in that passage? Why does Paul repeat them? Where is Philippi? Who was Paul's first convert?

They've read the passage, so they know most of the answers. But White's rapid-fire questioning makes for a jerky conversation. "These Philippians were his babies," White says. "We might just read about that. Acts 16." He points out that the narration of the Acts passage is in the first person. "Notice that 'we,'" he says. "Some people think that Luke, who wrote the book of Acts, may be giving a firsthand account." The jailer's whole family is baptized, he notes, and "that's an argument for infant baptism."

Everywhere he turns, he seems to find something else he needs to explain. Finally, though, he gets to the hymn in Philippians 2—the intended text. He scribbles a bunch of dates on the blackboard. Paul wrote in 50 A.D.; the first Gospel was written in 65. "If Paul's writing this passage from Ephesus, it's probably about 54, but if from Rome, it's the early '60s."

"You define this as a hymn," says Nancy, a middle-aged woman. "This was something that was sung?"

"Very likely," White says. "Does anyone know what lining out a hymn was?" He leads them in the first verse of "Shall We Gather at the River."

"Later," says Donald, a retired professor, "it became a bouncing ball."

"What is the first statement of faith in this hymn?" White asks with a mischievous grin. He seems to know this is going to confuse them; the UCC is not big on creeds. They offer him, indiscriminately, every line in the passage. Finally, almost by elimination, somebody suggests "Jesus Christ is Lord?"

"Where else have we heard that?" White asks. "In John," says Donald.

"At Caesarea Philippi," White says. "Remember Jesus says, 'Who do you say that I am?' and Peter says, 'You are the Christ'"? Almost on cue, they burst into a chorus from *Jesus Christ Superstar:* "So you are the Christ, the great Jesus Christ. . . . "

White asks for titles given to Jesus, and they come up with a long list: teacher, rabbi, savior, Joseph's son, Mary's son, shepherd, Lord, Christ. "What does Christ mean?" he asks.

"King, ruler," says Robert, a retired minister.

"But when I think of 'Lord,' I think domineering and feudal," says Eleanor, a teenager confirmed at the church a few months earlier. "What do they mean by 'Lord' here?"

White tries to make the concept palatable. "Messiah means 'anointed.' Anointed by whom? By God, and if by God, then 'special, set aside, empowered by the Almighty.'"

"Weren't his followers also thinking of him as a secular power who was going to save the Jewish people?" asks Robert. "His movement started not having so much religious as secular feeling, and people didn't realize he was the son of God until he was crucified."

"He never said he was son of God, did he?" asks Eleanor.

"You're raising an important question," says White. "We get all this son of God talk from John." Mentioning John leads him to the conflicts between Gentiles and Jews in the early church. In surveys they filled out as part of the project, many of these people said they don't study the Bible more than once a year, if that. Now that he's got them here, White seems to want to stuff everything he can into them.

"The way the Gospel was written," he says, "it ought to be read not as the story of the life of Jesus, but the story of the conflicts of the early church trying to find out who Jesus is."

"Say one more time?" asks a bewildered Nancy.

"The early church was using Jesus stories to define who they are. And we have in this passage all the conflicts that are going to appear. The passage saying Jesus is Lord is a real high concept of Jesus."

"This is something I've struggled with," she responds. "If Jesus is God, not different and separate from God, it seems like the sacrifice changes. It's easier to give yourself than to give your son. When you talk about Jesus was God, that relationship gets all goofed up for me."

"It's kind of God," says Eleanor. "Not God, but kind of."

"At the cross, the human died, but he still remained God," says Daniel.

"No, he remained humanity in God," insists Robert.

Nancy is still fretting. "I can't think of any scripture that puts Jesus and God all in one. God as a parent giving up his son for us seems the essence of sacrifice. He so loved the world that he gave himself? No—he gave his *son.*"

"That was added to the story afterwards, anyway," says Robert. "It was done to make it conform to the Old Testament. Jesus became God's lamb."

White tries to smooth out the debate. "The Bible and the Christian church struggle all the time to find images that communicate about this man. No one in Jesus' time said this is Jesus Christ, as if Christ was his last name. That got attached as they looked back later and tried to figure it out."

"I think that's why this hymn is here," says Robert. "Paul says, 'I can't say how it is, but here is this hymn everyone knows, so let's sing it.'"

The conversation turns to hymns they know and love—or hate. "'He walks with me and he talks with me' is everybody's favorite hymn, I know, but I think it's an abomination," White says.

"I have another thought," says Robert. "There's a great poem of Emily Dickinson's, and now I understand it: 'Tell the truth but tell it slant.'"

"Oh," says Nancy, "I think I'm finally getting a handle on it. After Jesus was crucified, there must have been a lot of chaos."

"Big time," says White.

"Truth must dazzle gradually," says Robert, quoting Dickinson again.

"It's a good reason to go to Bible study," says Nancy, "to get just a little bit of it."

The official text next week is Acts 8:26–40: the story of the Ethiopian eunuch converted by Philip. White starts with a structural outline of the New Testament: the Gospels, Acts, the epistles ("the wives of the apostles," he jokes), Revelation. He stages the Acts story as a little play. Nancy, cast as the eunuch, provokes gales of laughter by adopting a tinny, high-pitched voice.

"Is the eunuch the first Gentile to become a Christian?" White asks.

"What about the Canaanite woman?" says Nancy.

"She wasn't necessarily a Christian," White says.

"Since the eunuch was going to Jerusalem, don't we assume he was already a Christian?" asks Eleanor.

"No, he was a Jew," Richard says.

"Can he be a Jew?" White asks, reading Deuteronomy 23:1, which says that no one whose testicles are crushed or whose penis is cut off can be admitted to the assembly of the Lord.

I am beginning to lose my patience with White's Socratic approach; he seems to me to be trying to dig out of them facts they simply don't know. He'd save a lot of time if he just explained that the eunuch was probably a so-called "God-fearer," a Gentile who followed Jewish practices without undergoing circumcision.

But he has something else in mind. "The question is whether a person was made a eunuch or could be born one. If they were born, were they homosexual? These are the kinds of little questions you have to raise."

He goes on to argue that, if most of the Gentiles in the temple were eunuchs (read homosexuals), then perhaps what Jesus was doing when he drove the money-changers out was defending gay people. "I'm really stretching this, aren't I?" But his audience is eating it up.

"This eunuch was probably a seeker," White goes on, "and he wasn't accepted in the temple, so his mind is in a quandary. He's reading the book of Isaiah, and he turns to chapter 56, about eunuchs being welcomed in. Isaiah was a different cat; he'd welcome eunuchs."

The text, however, forces White to drop his suppositions; the passage the eunuch is described as reading is not from chapter 56, but from chapter 53, one of the mysterious "suffering servant" songs that the early Christians applied to Jesus. White has members of the class read the passage first as it occurs in Isaiah and then as it is quoted in Acts. Their translations are so different that there's little to be learned from the exercise.

"If you had to guess, who do you think Isaiah is talking about?" asks White. "Jesus," respond a couple of voices.

"Clearly the writer of Acts is saying it refers to Jesus," White says, "but the person who wrote Isaiah could be talking about the Jews and their future fate if they didn't change their ways."

It is not possible, I think in frustration, to address Isaiah's theology *and* Luke's theology *and* the views of Jesus and the early church on homosexuals, in an hour and a half.

White starts talking about a Christian-Jewish dialogue he recently attended. "No Jew ever thought of the messiah as somebody who was going to suffer," he says. "We ought to buy that PBS series on *From Jesus to Christ*—wasn't that great? Christians had to make sense of Jesus' death, and discovered that in the Bible are passages about a person who suffered in silence and was forsaken by others, and they began to say maybe the messiah wasn't like we ever thought about him. Maybe he was like this suffering servant."

"The eunuch has been made an outcast and found this passage very attractive," says Robert. "He's cut off from the world of living men. This is the hinge of the whole story."

"I think you're onto something," White says.

"It's never dealt with in the story, but it's a tantalizing subtext."

"He is baptized," White says. "What would baptism mean to him?"

"His alienation is over."

"We are stepping closer and closer to the mission to the Gentiles," says White, "and that's the point I'm trying to get our heads around. Always the Christian church has struggled with how the gift of God gets transferred from Jews to Gentiles."

"The early church was antitemple, too." Robert has wound White's imaginings inextricably into the story. "Look what they did to the Ethiopian in the temple."

"We are dealing with issues in the Hebrew Bible and reading them from a Christian script," White says. "How does the spirit of God work in this, and with us, and with the Bible?"

"We can all identify with it," says Donald. "We feel like that eunuch."

The idea that the eunuch had been rejected from the temple may be a stretch, but it is what allows the story to speak to them. They are liberal Christians in a town where conservative Christianity runs rampant; in Colorado Springs, the word "Christian" is not understood to include them.

"I just love it," says Nancy, "that feeling of 'Hey, I'm OK; God spoke to me directly; this is about me.'"

"Do you want to speculate further about what the spirit of God is doing?" White asks her.

"No—I just felt really good once you'd done explaining it. I could feel God's love."

"I don't know," says White, "if mainline Protestants read the Bible to hear the word of God, or think the Spirit is going to speak to them through the Bible. Do any of you take that tack?"

He seems to have lost steam on Acts, and I wonder if he is heading in this direction because I am here.

"I get embarrassed by characters waiting to be led by the Spirit and flopping open the page," says Donald. "It's Bible roulette."

"You say you're flipping the pages," says Nancy. "What if somebody is causing them to open where they do?"

"It's roulette," he says stubbornly.

"No, it's predestination," she says.

White recalls a time when he was without a job, in an uncertain marriage, and anxious. "I ran across a passage that said God will keep him in perfect peace whose mind is stayed on him, and I took that as a kind of revelation."

"Was it random?" asks Donald.

"I've had that happen," says Nancy. "I do think it's a little freaky."

"Or is it a question of when the student is ready, the teacher will appear?" asks White's wife. "You could have read it ten times before, and it didn't mean what it did that day."

"Like when the eunuch was ready for Philip," Nancy says. "If you prepare yourself by studying the Bible, it will happen."

That's hard to do, argues Tom, who hadn't been there last week. "In the twentieth century, the Bible isn't viewed as inspired or religious. It requires a leap of faith for people just to study it seriously, because they see so many contradictory passages and messages."

That's not a problem for fundamentalists, notes White.

"It's very similar to the Constitution," Tom says. "It can mean anything you want it to mean."

"I always wonder why the Bible is so difficult," says Nancy. "Wasn't it meant for a person of average intelligence?"

It was, White tells her.

"Then why is it so hard to read and understand?"

Hovering in the background of both evenings' conversations is the unnamed other, the conservative Christians in whose territory they feel themselves to be resident aliens. It seems to me that White is trying, through his digressions and his historical speculations, to give his people a sense that they too own the Bible, that they too can relate, in some way, to the book the conservatives seem to have claimed for their own.

But it is hard going. Most of the people in this group know about the Bible only what they have heard in church, or absorbed from their families, or picked up in the media—an only half-thought-out amalgam of Sunday school stories, liberal senti-

ments, and a distaste for Bible-thumpers. They have little in the
way of context in which to place the facts and ideas White has
been firing at them. No wonder they are confused.

When I talked to White, I could hear the frustration spurting
out of him. He told me a story about leading church members in
a song he'd learned as a child. "There was a verse that went 'Esau
was a cowboy of the wild and woolly make; half the farm
belonged to him and half belonged to Jake.' People had no idea
what that was about, who Esau was, or Jake, or what the sandwich and bottle of beer was referring to. It was a big blank.

"When I offer a Bible study," he went on, "if I can get a dozen
people out, I feel really lucky. But I woke up one morning not
long ago and realized that over a two-week period, we had
spawned not one, not two, but *three* dream groups that any number of people would come out for. People believe more in the
truth of the collective subconscious than in the revealed word of
God. They believe if they can just tap the divine child or the great
mother inside of them, they are going to find truth."

White blames a culture of individualism with which he sees
himself at war. "That me-and-Jesus intimacy is not right. Not
right. Faith is not just about me and my maker, it's about us and
the Lord. The Bible is a book for communal purposes: from faith
to faith, from the people of God in the early church to the people of God in the contemporary church."

But he lives with the knowledge that this is not what his congregation is seeking. "We are cultural Protestants, and what people are looking for is an inspiring moment. We want to have our
kids in Sunday school and out of our hair; we want some kind of
infusion of spirituality; and we want the sense that we belong."

White's scattershot conversation is accompanied by an engag-
ing humility. "God, listen to me talking like I know something,"
he said at one point—and went right on doing it. "We are all trying to create some sort of feeling of me and God-ness that
touches our beat-up little psyches and gives them comfort. And
then we want our psyches to be warmed by other psyches, like

when the kids from the blind choir come in and sing 'Amazing Grace' and your heart is just torn up."

"Yeah, I would like to give them more if they would take it," he said. "I would like to give them a commitment to the realization of the reign of God. I think if we were really committed to the kingdom of God, we would be more passionately concerned about the welfare of our brothers and sisters in the world."

Church members sometimes complain that White, with his strong social passion, scants more spiritual concerns. The charge annoys him; but it is true that he is more comfortable with contemplative prayer than with prayer based on scripture. "I don't believe the Bible is the revealed word of God," he said. "The word of God is Christ. I can't invest the Bible with the magic that conservatives or evangelicals do."

But he insisted conservatives who accuse him of being unbiblical have it wrong. "I continually say to people that I take the Bible much too seriously to take it literally. But most of the time they hear that I don't take it literally, without hearing that I take it seriously. But the purpose of the Bible is not to get us to heaven; it is to help us to think about how we live in relation with God and neighbor—and that's a *we*."

White's scriptural spins aren't limited to making the Ethiopian eunuch a gay man. A few weeks earlier, he told me, he'd been thinking about one of the more unpleasant stories about Jesus— the story in which he not only refuses a Canaanite woman's request to heal her daughter, but insults her to boot, saying it's not fair to give the bread intended for Israelites to dogs.

"But she just badgers him to where he finally has to pay attention," White says, "and he's impressed with her faith and does it. I got to thinking that this woman is like God. God is coming to us and saying, 'Take care of my child, the earth.' But we don't want to hear that, so God says, 'I'm going to badger you about this until you pay attention.' I think scripture is a way of opening us to new possibilities."

Listening to White, I got the feeling that his passion for the Bible, deep as it is, is somehow cut off from the book itself. That what he loves is not what's in the pages but what he can make of what's in the pages.

Expanding the biblical stories is an age-old way of reading the book, going back to the rabbis who filled in the blanks in Abraham's conversations with God. But in the classes I'd visited, as well as my conversation with White, the expansions and digressions seemed more a way of dodging the text than of entering into it.

But what else could they do? For almost everyone I'd met in those two evenings, truth was to be found not in the book in front of them but in those dates and outlines White had written on the board. They knew Jesus had not been born of a virgin; what then were they to make of a book that says he was? Out of such a book, God's voice *can* come only through a kind of superstitious magic. No wonder many of them said in their surveys that they thought the Bible should be expanded, and even more wanted to see it revised. When the book on which your faith is based becomes something you have to explain away, where do you turn?

Chapter 3

Pax Christi Retreat

Huntington, NY

W e are in a room deep in the basement of an old seminary, now used as a retreat house. The walls and ceiling are covered with pipes and wires. The furniture looks as though it's been put down here as the last stop before the dump.

It's a good place for revolutionaries—which is what Ched Myers, the leader of this weekend workshop, would like to turn us into. I am sitting in on the annual retreat of the New York chapter of Pax Christi, the Roman Catholic peace group. "Is there going to be Bible study on this retreat?" I had asked Myers when I met him in California. "There is *always* Bible study on my retreats," he replied. "That's what I do."

I first came across Myers about twenty years ago, in the pages of *Sojourners*, one of the main journals of the Christian peace and justice movement and the first explicitly Christian magazine I had ever read. Myers, whom conservatives would call communist if they had ever heard of him, is a frequent *Sojourners* contributor, and when I first started reading the Bible, it was through his lens as much as anyone's. For someone ensconced, as I was and am, in the comfortably off middle class, it's not a comfortable perspective; I spent the first few years of my active Christian life fending off guilt over working for *The Wall Street Journal* instead of the *Catholic Worker*.

41

It's the first weekend in Lent, so Myers hangs his retreat around the readings for Ash Wednesday. (It's also in the midst of renewed U.S. bombing in Iraq, a topic that comes up over and over during the weekend.) Myers tells us about getting ashes in a church where he had to step around and over poor folk to get in. "I heard the readings in a new way."

Myers is trying to do two things this weekend: explicate the Bible and create and nourish community. In theory, the two are practically synonymous, at least by his reading of the Bible. In practice, they sometimes fit oddly together.

He covers a low table with a beautiful piece of South American weaving, puts a candle on it, and leads us in song. Then he starts telling us about the city Jonah was running away from when he ended up in the whale's belly. "Nineveh was the capital of Assyria," he says, "and Assyria was Israel's mortal enemy. It was this incredible imperial force that had rolled over them, raped and pillaged and carted them off."

So no wonder, he says, Jonah didn't want God forgiving them—especially through his preaching. "The biblical stories are talking about master symbols of the human condition," Myers says, "big people kicking the bejesus out of little people. The challenge is, what are your options? One is you can return hatred for hatred even if you can't kick them back, and two is that you can tell the big people the truth about themselves—not a very popular vocation. Jonah is a parable of nonviolence."

His rhythms and cadences are those of the southern preacher: vivid, folksy, and often very funny. "I wouldn't piss on you if you were on fire," he imagines Jonah saying to the Ninevites.

The Jonah story is echoed, he says, in the Gospel story of Jesus calming the storm. "The journey of repentance doesn't take us into quiet inner sanctums of spiritual bliss, but into the heart of the storm."

"Sometimes we don't trust people's true repentance," says a man in the group. "What would we do if Clinton repented? Would we think we'd done a good job, or would we sit around saying you can't trust a politician?"

"Keep in mind," Myers responds, "that the book of Jonah was written to an oppressed people who have no experience of an oppressor repenting. Let's not get too sentimental here; this is a tough book written in the teeth of a world where the probability of Nineveh repenting is not high."

At the end of the session, they hold hands and pray.

When I talk to Myers after the session, he hugs me, touches my arm, asks about my life and my feelings. I feel the way I imagine my dog does when somebody moves too quickly to pet her. I feel as if I'm being co-opted, as if he assumes that because I've written for *Mother Jones* and, a few times, for *Sojourners,* we are on the same team. We're not.

At breakfast the next morning I hear a lot of talk about Iraq, about the sinfulness of trying to defend the American lifestyle, about how painful it is when your country is the bad guy. I sympathize with, and to some extent, share, those feelings. But it also strikes me that these folks, many of them nuns, live in a cocoon. They don't seem to recognize the insecurities flying around the American psyche: fears of being downsized, of having to watch your children settle for second best because life isn't what it used to be. Choosing poverty, as so many of these people have done, is very different from having it forced upon you.

What did they make of Jonah? Myers asks.

"What I heard was that we are called not just to turn around ourselves, but to go to those who are oppressing and speak truth to them," says one woman.

"I identified most with the fear Jonah had," says another. "He ran away. That's why I admire groups like Pax Christi so much. They give you courage."

Myers starts talking about the last war on Iraq, Desert Storm. "I want us to come back to that in order to feel in our guts what we are talking about when we talk about struggling to turn the historical direction around. Do you remember what it felt like to be in the midst of what can only be described as war mania?"

"I was in Pakistan in the Peace Corps," says a woman in a blue shirt who begins to cry as she tells the story, "and the American embassy said we had to leave. We arrived at Kennedy Airport and

were greeted by officials waving flags and saying, 'Isn't this wonderful?' And we didn't want to be here."

""When I heard about smart bombs," confesses another
woman, "I found it very exciting. I could feel myself drawn in."

"What bothered me," says a man in the group, "was a Saturday morning TV news special with kids gathered around talking
about why we are bombing people. One kid raised her hand and
said, 'Are we killing children?' and they cut to a commercial."

The responses are pouring out. Myers tries to stem the flow,
but the group insists on going on, and he yields. When the
stories finally tail off, he begins singing the song with which he
had started the session. "And when I rise, let me rise up like a
bird. . . ."

"The moment of wartime," he says, "is the time to fish or cut
bait. But it's too late, because the fish has become a whale, and
we're in its belly, and how do you fish for a monster in the belly
of which you dwell?

"We need to learn to live in sobriety," he says, "from the war
mania that's always just under the surface of the American
empire. We need the kind of love that loves enough to intervene.
We also have to have resources, and one of the great founts of
those is scripture."

The story he's dealing with this morning is Jesus' temptation
in the wilderness. "We want to talk about the radical journey of
Jesus," he says. "At the roots of our tradition are some very old
stories, and they are wiser than we are. Jesus is setting a primal
pattern by taking a journey back to his roots."

Jesus was doing what Moses did, he says. "The Israelites were
called to be in recovery from the addictive, compulsive system of
slavery in Egypt. They have no clue how to do that. How would
they? They grew up watching Egyptian television; they went to
Egyptian schools. That's why they have to spend forty years
learning to live in an other-than-Egypt manner. It's all about getting the hell out of Dodge.

"We Christians have a fabulous capacity to trivialize the
Hebrew Bible," he says. "We say the Old Testament is just a
bunch of rules and regulations. We don't understand that every

single instruction in the Torah is trying to teach people to be non-Egyptians, and lesson number one, the first thing you have to learn, is how to operate the economy in a way that's not going to rebuild Egypt. It's the economy, stupid."

That's the point of the first temptation, he says; when Jesus refuses to turn stones into bread, he is saying that in God's economy, everything comes from God and we all get what we need.

"Then the devil showed him all the kingdoms of the world, as if to show him 'you've seen one, you've seen 'em all. They all work the same way, and here's the kicker—I own it.'" Myers is playing the devil, and relishing it. "But for you I'll make such a deal. . . ."

God is king, Myers says, jumping to the story in Samuel of the Israelites wanting a king, like all the nations around them. "'You tell them, Samuel,' God says, 'what they're going to get along with it. They'll get taxes, conscription, a standing military, a political economic aparatus in which wealth trickles upward and the economy is geared to the elite.'"

Myers is only telling half the story. Intertwined with the book's conviction that human kingship is wrong is a triumphant paean to the glories of David's reign. Whoever put together the final version of the story embraced both points of view in an unresolved and complex tension.

Psalm 91, which the devil quotes in the third temptation, is a favorite of military chaplains, Myers says. "The devil says God isn't going to let anything harm you. And this is the heart of the matter, the thing that allows all the economics of inequality to go unchallenged. It hooks into the spirit of entitlement."

The point of Jesus' response is that it's not God being tested, it's us. "We get it wrong when God becomes the patron saint of our projects. All the Bible promises is a rough journey."

My first clear recognition of the contrariness of my own nature came from reading William Shirer's *The Rise and Fall of the Third Reich*. By the time I was a quarter of the way through, Shirer's constant reminders of how terrible Hitler was were getting on my nerves. I was beginning to think that nobody, even Hitler, could have been *that* bad—at which point I decided the book was bad for my character and threw it away. Myers is having something of the same effect on me. It's not that I disagree with him. But I wish that, like the writers of this book he so admires, he would make room for the opposition.

No such luck. "There's only one story," he tells this group after leading them in an old spiritual. "The question is, How are we going to tell it today? The Bible gets trivialized in the pulpit or fetishized in academia where it's treated like an artifact to examine. The reason I like to sing is to remind us that the thing the Bible is most like is a piece of music. A musical score wants to be played. The Bible wants to come to life, and it only comes to life when people say this story tells the truth about the world."

Myers has earned the right to criticize the academic approach to scripture; his best-known book, *Binding the Strong Man,* a political and economic analysis of Mark's Gospel, started life as a master's thesis at Berkeley Divinity School.

Myers had been a peace activist and a halfhearted Christian for several years, he told me, before he encountered the radical Christian tradition. He attended a seminar on the Sermon on the Mount where the speaker raised the question, What if Jesus really meant what he said?

"It was part huge relief, and part firecrackers going off," Myers said of his reaction. "Here, in this tradition that I'd been intuitively drawn to but that kept disappointing me, was this call to a radical lifestyle, to a transforming engagement. Here was a story that offered an alternative to the world's story. It was my conversion to the gospel." Within a year, he was living, and protesting, with Daniel Berrigan and Elizabeth McAllister. "That was how I got midwifed into this little floating crap game we call radical Christianity in America. And through it all, the thing that kept interesting me was the scripture part."

Listening to Myers talk about scripture—which, given a chance, he will do for hours—is an experience somewhat akin to watching the movie *All of Me,* in which Steve Martin's body is simultaneously occupied by Martin and by Lily Tomlin. Only in this case, you're listening to Shirley MacLaine and Michel Foucault.

"In the early '80s, when I was in seminary, a lot of stuff that

was routinely talked about on liberal campuses, like social loca-
tion, race, class, and gender, were nowhere. I was asking two sets
of questions. One, what is the political context for these stories?
What are the encoded social and political strategies? And two,
why are we reading and picking apart these stories as if they were
potsherds? Why don't we look at them as narratives, with
integrity?

"If we want to change the world," he went on, "we're going to
have to find a way for people to be reenfranchised to read these
stories. We believe we are smarter than they were two thousand
years ago. But what if we're wrong? What if in fact we've fallen
further down the hole? Everybody says, What about the atom,
what about modern dentistry and penicillin? But what if traditional people, who say the older it is, the wiser it is—what if
they're right? What if modern technology can't rescue the text
for us? What if the problem doesn't lie with the stories, but with
us? What if this book is not so much something we need to control, as something we need to yield to? Modern exegesis is like
running these stories through a mill, dismantling, pulling apart
and remanufacturing them, and out the other end comes a little
ingot of 'truth.' Well, what does that sound like? Sounds like
industrial capitalism to me. Of course any sociologist of knowledge will say, 'Big surprise.' But the question is, Is this what we
are supposed to be doing to sacred texts?"

When I got my first really big raise, years and years ago, the
first thing I did was go up to Burberry's on Fifty-seventh Street
to buy a top-of-the-line reporter's trench coat. On my way up
Madison Avenue, I passed a youngish, plainly dressed woman
standing in a doorway, holding up a sign asking for help. Those
signs have since become commonplace in New York, but this was
the first one I had ever seen. And for a few moments I could not
endure the fact that she was standing there too beaten-down
even to speak, and I was on my way to spend five hundred dollars on a coat.

I bought the coat anyway. But those are the strings that get
tugged when I listen to Myers. I have spent my professional life
dancing between God and mammon. I write about Wall Street,

and I try to be a faithful Christian. It is a complicated path, filled with irony and demanding, I often feel, the judgment of Solomon. If I were to buy into Myers's vision, I would escape a lot of those complexities.

Myers does not talk, as Billy Graham does, about heaven and hell. He doesn't threaten people who don't buy his ideas with eternal torment. But he is in no doubt that they are wrong; that they are, if not enemies of God themselves, then servants of the enemies of God. They are following idols—and to follow idols is, in biblical language, to choose death.

Judging by the reactions to Myers's presentations, though, I'm an oddity here. The people in this room have spent years, many of them, waging what has often seemed an utterly fruitless campaign to end war. They need the succor of knowing they are on God's side as much as Billy Graham's listeners need the assurance of heaven.

At the end of the weekend, Myers asks them where they fit into this story.

"I am compulsive about money," says a woman with curly white hair. "I get sick and I run out and get a two-hundred-dollar dress. I made a vow of poverty, and I feel safer, but I don't think that's the answer, to feel safe."

"It's so easy to talk about things we feel on the right side of," says a young man. "But I'm very uncomfortable talking about racism because I haven't mastered it. It's part of my life and experience, and I'm not on the right side, and it's scary."

"It's not violence out there that concerns me," says a dark-haired, bearded man. "It's violence in my own heart. I am an angry person with a vicious tongue. You talk about life and death—this is death stuff for me. And addiction talk doesn't help. I can't go to an angry-tongues-anonymous meeting."

"I want my feeling of not being good enough to be loved to be addressed," says a young woman. "I know it's addressed in scripture—Jesus addresses it—but I bring it up in the peace movement and it's like drawing a blank. Not many people in the peace and justice movement know what it's like even to walk in their own shoes, much less mine."

She gets no response here, either.

After the weekend, I talked to two of the men who'd attended the retreat. Vinny Pisciotta, an advertising executive who's active with Saul Alinsky's Industrial Areas Foundation, signed up for the weekend because he admires Myers's book. Though he is a Roman Catholic, Pisciotta's most vivid exposure to the Bible came through the Intervarsity Christian Fellowship, an evangelically oriented group he became involved with in college. "They taught us to look for themes and connections," he said, "for two stories that may bookend a story between them. I also learned how much of the New Testament is a revisioning of the Old Testament. I don't know where they stood on biblical infallibility. They would say it's all useful; is it necessarily designed to be perfectly historically accurate? I would say no, and I think they would. Much more important than that is how it is woven together to speak to you and your experience right now."

For Pisciotta, Myers's approach brought a missing dimension to the Bible. "There was something that had bugged me but I had never been able to put my finger on—the step of faith that goes beyond how I am doing with God, my own growth and enrichment and learning to be a 'better person.' And once it's pointed out, you can't miss it—how impressive Jesus was with his own authority in defending the downtrodden, the oppressed, people at the mercy of those in power."

From reading Myers, Pisciotta says, he learned to hear the questions Jesus asks the disciples as questions to him. "Jesus asks, Who do you say that I am? and Peter gives the right answer but doesn't know what it means. It's about suffering and alliance with those who suffer, about a lot of stuff we still have to keep reminding ourselves about over and over, because everything around us tells us that life is about money, and power, and fame. Our job in life is, if we can buy a nicer house, to do it; if we can send our kids to a better school, do it. But maybe life is about wondering why everyone else isn't invited to this party? If life is an ever-ascending party in the palace, then nine-tenths of the people in the world aren't invited. That makes extra-insightful the analogy between Peter as a disciple and Peter the modern-day Christian, wanting to follow Jesus and following him into the courtyard where he knows Jesus is being interrogated and beaten and suffering at the hands of the powers. But Peter is paralyzed on the other side of the wall, to save his ass. Is that us?"

Pisciotta and his family live comfortably in a Long Island suburb, and I asked whether, given his reading of the Bible, he's at ease with that. He gave me an embarrassed grin. "I'm always walking a fine line between being too hard on myself and too easy on myself. What my dad was earning at the end of his career, I've far surpassed in the first third of mine. Now I have to view my circumstances and my choices in terms of my understanding of who I am and where my treasure is." He's also married, with kids, and his wife doesn't see things exactly the same way.

But he does what he can, he says. Given Jesus' words about laying up treasure on earth, he's not sure he should have a 401(k), but he does. But he has put it in a socially responsible mutual fund. "People my age are always being told they are going to need several hundred thousand dollars to send their kids to college, and they get frightened and believe that unless they start doubling what they've got, the kid has no future. But I will not be intimidated. I'm pretty good at having a perspective on what money is for. But I'm better on wealth than I am on possessions. I like stuff."

Keith Kessler had never even heard of Myers until the retreat. "I went there to go on retreat," he said. "I didn't even bring a Bible."

Kessler also suffers from an attention disorder that kept him from remembering much about the weekend, even just a few days later. So we talked instead about the Bible, which he reads constantly. "Unless something grips my attention, I can't read it. The Bible does. Whenever I open it to explore it, I encounter God. Period, end of story."

Kessler is not a fundamentalist. "Each Gospel spins Jesus in a different way," he says. "But one thing that's clear is the times when he gets really angry and threatens divine retribution are always around hypocrisy or suffering."

I asked him if the Bible gave him a sense of what Jesus really was like. "I hope I'm not that naive," he said quickly. Then he paused, and grinned. "Yeah, I am that naive, although I hope I would have some skepticism."

Certainly he's encountered skepticism; a while back he joined a MENSA Bible group that promised interdenominational discussion. "But when I got there, it was a guy trying to tear the Bible apart. He asked really probing questions about what kind of a God is this, questions that really challenged my faith and got me to concede that some things in the Bible are silly and stupid."

The Bible wasn't written just for scholars, Kessler says passionately; he has taught it to retarded children. "If you believe it is the inspired word of God, it was given to every human being, no matter what their talent and capacity and ability to understand and interpret. For those who can't understand words, it can be expressed in music or pictures.

"I need scholars," he went on. "I may be dense, but I read Mark dozens of times before I realized Jesus was very lonely, or that a big theme is the Messianic secret. I need scholars to hit me over the head with that. But I also need people who are walking through searing pain, and the only thing they can hold onto is God speaking to them through the Bible."

Kessler is willing, it seems, to take God anywhere he can find him. But he confesses that he had a hard time with Myers. "He talked an awful lot about money, and I wished he would stop, because he was putting me on edge." Partly that's because he was stirring up some guilt, Kessler explained. "I have this dilemma, that since I get disability, I make more money by not working than I could by working. Any way you slice it, that's wrong. His talking about money that weekend got me thinking about how I am going to address this inequity."

Is it inequity? Kessler's conversation shines with intelligence and even wisdom, but it also jumps around in a way that made me wonder whether he could, in fact, hold a job. Is he, in Myers's scheme of things, participating in injustice by taking benefits to which he is entitled? Maybe I'm just trying to get myself off the hook, but it seems to me that guilt plays a powerful role in Myers's appeal—to me as well as to Kessler. One of the rewards of throwing yourself into the cannon's mouth, after all, is that you no longer have to wonder whether you have done your utmost.

Chapter 4

Myers Park Baptist Church

Charlotte, NC

B ill Dols, the education minister at Myers Park Baptist
  Church, in Charlotte, North Carolina, is introducing
tonight's speaker. "There are saluters and searchers," Dols says;
saluters hold to creeds while searchers are looking for Jesus. Walter Wink is a searcher.

In an era in which the Southern Baptists have come to represent all that liberals dislike most about conservative Christians,
the idea of a liberal Baptist church seems an oxymoron. But
Myers Park is as liberal as they come. At Myers Park, the word
"creed" comes with a sneer attached. The congregation was
thrown out of the local Baptist Association because it doesn't
require immersion, and stalked out of the Southern Baptist Conference when the conservatives took it over. "They would
describe themselves as being true Baptists," Dols told me. "No
minister or priest is going to tell them what to do."

Myers Park has invited Wink and his wife, June Keener-Wink,
to do a weekend workshop, and they're kicking it off with what
they describe as a dialogue: Wink and the interim dean of the
Belk College of Business Administration at the University of
North Carolina.

Walter Wink is a hard man to categorize. He was denied

tenure at Union Theological Seminary because of his touchy-feely teaching style, but his best-known work is a scholarly three-volume treatise on the doctrine of the principalities and powers. He's a radical pacifist and a profound believer in the practical efficacy of prayer, a friend of both Ched Myers and the deeply conservative Peter Wagner.

Right now he's talking about the angels of the churches to whom the letters that open the book of Revelation are addressed. "The letters are clearly to the congregations," he says, "but they're addressed to the angel. How to hold these two together? What finally came clear to me is that the angel is an actual spirit at the heart of the congregation." Every institution, every organization, every family, has an angel, he says.

There's another striking fact, he goes on: the congregations to which the author of Revelation writes are not all good: "When the angel of a church abandons its divine vocation, it becomes demonic. Remember the terrible saying of Jesus that not everyone who says 'Lord, Lord' will enter the kingdom? They were casting out demons and prophesying and doing mighty works, but they hadn't inquired of God what they were supposed to be doing, so God says, 'I never knew you.'"

Businesses have angels too, Wink says, and to change a business, you need to pay attention to its angel as well as its organization chart: "The angel acts like a homeostatic holding pattern, and it can absorb and sustain changes in personnel. You have to transform that spirit. Within the context of changing churches, intercessory prayer is very important. I am beginning to suspect that if you're trying to change the angel of a business, you'd better be praying pretty hard too."

He laughs at his own punch lines, but nobody laughs with him. I suspect they're a bit overwhelmed. Angels? Business? Homeostatic holding patterns?

Certainly the dean doesn't get it. He starts talking about the civic-minded business leaders Charlotte has been blessed with. Yes, corporations have personalities, he says. "But they come from two sources, leadership and personnel."

He talks about a class on business ethics in which 80 percent of the students freely admitted they'd cheat on an exam if they could get away with it. "That's the group you have to focus on for redemption," he says. "There is always the potential for corruption, but I think business can be noted for the good it does." Wink follows his lead, and the conversation quickly turns more conventional; they talk about corporate salaries, sweatshops, overseas investment. No angels.

When they ask for questions, a middle-aged man in a windbreaker is quick to stand up. "The pope of the Catholic Church recently indicated displeasure with capitalism because it fails people in third-world countries. I'm a business owner, and I attempt to run my business on a spiritual, though not a religious, basis. My question is, how can we respond to help this confused Catholic leader understand and appreciate the powers of capitalism? Capitalism hasn't failed those people; the thugs of those countries have failed them."

"I think we have to be careful of talking about the ethics of capitalism or communism," responds the dean, citing some notorious examples of irresponsible corporate behavior. "I think capitalism can be as ethical or unethical as business leaders want it to be."

"I listened to you on the radio today," says another questioner to Wink, "and I dispute your contention that nonviolence is effective. The Vietnam War dragged on for seventeen years, and it was politics that ended it, not all these morality plays."

"It's important to recognize that electoral politics is also a form of nonviolence," he responds.

I am longing for some fireworks; everyone is being painfully polite.

"Neither of you has mentioned Jesus," says a man who I later discover is the chairman of the church's board of deacons. "What would Jesus say if he had ten minutes in the boardroom at Bank of America?" This is a hot topic; NationsBank, a local institution, recently took over Bank of America, and the two companies were having a hard time getting along. The audience cheers. Wink gestures to the dean to take the question. The dean mimes walking away and then says, "Next question."

Reminds me of Pilate washing his hands—and just when it looked like it might get interesting.

Unless his wife can't be there (Wink himself, as he is about to make abundantly clear, is no dancer), all of Wink's workshops include movement. So on Saturday morning, the couple hauls the forty people gathered in the church basement to their feet. They're an odd pair: Walter tall and gangly, with whitening blond hair and aging-movie-star good looks; June small and dark, with a shy, narrow face. There is something distanced about the way they work together; right now, for instance, they are taking turns speaking, Keener-Wink in a kind of chant, Wink in a colloquial, almost jokey tone.

June: "Our bodies are our stories. We can't imagine a tomorrow without our bodies. We can't imagine a world free of violence without imagining our bodies safe."

Walter: "I have felt the importance of getting the body involved in Bible study since I was nineteen, when at camp they put on the Lord's Prayer and asked us to move. I ordered my body to move and it said 'no.' I said, 'Oh, yes.' It moved—reluctantly. I said, 'You're supposed to enjoy this.' It said, 'I'm not enjoying this one bit.' That was the day I discovered my body was an atheist."

June: "The church has not been kind to the body. Such an attitude is unbiblical. There is no word in Hebrew for body or for soul; there is only one word, *nephesh*, all of me, my whole self, my aliveness."

Walter: "So when we do body work, what we're trying to do is incarnate scripture into flesh. The great cop-out in Christianity is the idea that only Jesus incarnated God, instead of realizing Jesus came to teach us how."

Keener-Wink gets everyone stretching, jumping, and acting out emotions. This is not a language in which this crowd is fluent, but they are game. Wink is bouncing up and down like the dork at the disco party. "Walter," someone said to me later in the day, "is not a movement person."

Keener-Wink brings the movement to an end and asks how it was. Happy and excited conversation breaks out all over the room. They were having fun.

The formal discussion begins with an imaginative evocation of two different stories of humanity's origin. Keener-Wink does the first, reading in a dreamy tone, accompanied by even dreamier music, an idyllic account of the earliest society. "War had not been invented," she says.

"War had not been invented," Wink echoes. Women were equal to men, and democracy was the norm. Before the domination system.

To Wink, the domination system—any system of government in which power depends on dominating others (which for him means any system at all except the primitive agrarian idyll just described)—is what Jesus came to free us from, the fundamental evil of the universe. His term for the kingdom of God is "God's domination-free order." So now the two of them tell the myth of the domination system, in rough, jerky voices and accompanied by noisy, cymbal-filled music. Wink takes the lead this time, his wife echoing him.

"In the beginning, Axu the father god and Tiamat the mother god gave birth to children, but the frolicking of the younger gods keeps their parents awake, so they decide to kill their children."

This is the Babylonian creation story, the one scholars believe the Genesis account was written to counter. The children get wind of their parents' plot and kill Axu. Tiamat swears revenge. The young gods turn to Marduk, the youngest, who says if they'll give him dominion, he'll save them. He kills Tiamat, scatters her blood, and out of her corpse creates a cosmos. He imprisons the gods that sided with Tiamat, except for one, whom he kills. Out of his blood, Marduk creates human beings to serve the gods.

"How did you feel about that story?" Wink asks.

There is only one answer to that question, and he gets it: it was brutal; the music made me feel anxious; a culture of fear; violence begets violence. I wonder if I am the only one here who feels manipulated.

Wink goes into a riff about how even cartoons reflect the domination system. Back during the God-is-dead furor, he says, he watched one theologian say on television that nobody could possibly believe in a Christ who physically descended from heaven to earth. "Then a cartoon came on, with Hercules sliding from heaven to earth on a thunderbolt, and the kids weren't having trouble with it at all. In cartoons, the bad guys lose, but in the next episode they're always back because they function like gods. They can't be destroyed. What is going on here is a passive understanding of salvation. You don't have to do anything—you simply accept it by identifying with the right side. This myth is tremendously powerful all around the world as an explanation for the way things really are. After the break, we're going to talk about Jesus' answer to the domination system."

Responding to the domination system, Wink tells us when we reconvene, was the entire message of Jesus' ministry. "I understand Jesus' gospel as a disease-specific remedy for the domination system." Indeed, he judges the truth of Jesus' reported sayings on the basis of whether they address the domination system. "If they do," he says in what might be a joke, "they're true whether Jesus said them or not."

He cites a host of examples: saying the last shall be first, teaching that you can't serve God and mammon, refusing to accept titles, washing his disciples' feet, entering Jerusalem on a donkey in what Wink says was a parody of Davidic kingship. "Jesus was not a minor reformer, but an egalitarian prophet who refutes the very premises on which domination is based—the right to lord it over others."

It all fits, he says. Jesus was down on families because the family is infested with patriarchy. His band of followers was scandalously mixed, including women without their husbands and men without their wives. Wink cites feminist scholars on the significance of Jesus' treatment of women. "Look at the story of Martha and Mary. Where's the anomaly? Mary is behaving like a male disciple. Martha is incensed, and instead of saying to Mary, 'Come help,' she goes to Jesus, playing the patriarchal system against her sister. Jesus says Mary has chosen the one thing that is important. It would have been good if he'd said, 'Let's all go into the kitchen and wash up and then we'll talk.' But he is violating an important social practice.

"The gospel, it turns out, is incredibly simple. It is the coming of God's domination-free order. Period." And why has nobody figured this out before? The church, he says, has been in cahoots with the dominators. "But the church's apostasy from the new order of Jesus mustn't blind us to what he is doing."

The audience is a pretty even mix of the sexes, but when Wink asks for questions, he hears almost entirely from women. And what they want to talk about, one way or another, is feminism. Why do you use God-father language? Aren't you idealizing the feminine? "Your use of feminine language for God in the Twenty-third Psalm brought tears to my eyes," says one woman.

"What hints can you give us on how to address the domination within ourselves?" asks another, adding pointedly, "and I'd like to hear June speak too."

She has put her finger on an inherent contradiction that runs through this workshop—for all the talk of turning systems upside down, Wink and his wife are playing very conventional roles. He does the hard, intellectual stuff; she does the soft, emotional stuff. He speaks; she supports. He talks to participants during the break; she sets up the equipment for the next session.

I am trying to pick holes in Wink's presentation, and I know it. I know why, too—he is making me angry. So much of what he says makes so much sense; he has, for instance, given me for the first time a vocabulary in which to talk about the demonic without embarrassment. I want to agree with him. But his insistence that he has found the single, all-encompassing explanation of every-thing in the Bible—"the gospel, period"—makes me feel pushed into opposition. Dols was wrong about Wink, I think. He's not searching for anything. He is damn certain he's found it.

At the start of the next session, Keener-Wink asks participants to imagine light coming as a blessing out of their fingertips. "Now move that light up to the universe; send that sparkle. Now, always leaving light where you've been, pull the light back to earth and bless the oceans, the rivers, the streams. Our domination system has polluted them and we are a part of it, so we want to pray for their healing. Bring that light to the soil that's been contaminated and overused. Now bring it back to this room and cover each other with light. Cover yourself with light. Give yourself a love bath. We've been taught not to touch ourselves. We've been taught that masturbation is wrong. We know it's not, but it has made so many of us so afraid to touch any part of ourselves. The commandment tells us to love our neighbors as ourselves. Can we do that until we love our body-selves, our *nephesh*? Take this wonderful permission to touch yourselves."

She distributes scarves, and they dance the Beatitudes, scarves waving in the air. In front of me, a middle-aged woman with a huge butt and triple chins is moving with impressive grounded-ness. When the movement ends, they burst into applause.

The afternoon workshop features the part of Wink's theory that is probably most widely quoted, at least on the Christian Left: his explication of Jesus' teaching on nonviolence. When my son was little, his Sunday school teacher devoted a session to the passage from Matthew that Wink is about to discuss: the injunc-tion not to resist evil, to turn the other cheek, to give your enemy even more than he takes from you, to go the extra mile. My son's conclusion? Jesus was nuts.

Wink asks the group to list its own responses. It turns us into doormats, comes one answer. The dominators win; it's not prac-tical; it hurts; it's humiliating. . . .

You're right, Wink says. "Christians, sensing something terri-bly wrong here, have quite wisely said this is a crock. Jesus resis-ted evil with all his might, so what does this mean?"

The word translated "resist," in the phrase "Do not resist evil," actually describes a technique of ancient warfare, he tells us— marching towards the enemy until you collide and then standing there fighting until one side breaks ranks. "Jesus is saying do not stand against evil on its own terms."

He calls for a volunteer. "When we hear the word 'strike,' most of us probably think about a right hook. But that hits the left cheek, not the right. A left hook will fit, but you can't use your left hand because it's not clean. So it has to be the back of your right hand. And that's always delivered by a superior to an infe-rior. It's a symbolic way of saying you've been uppity. So Jesus is saying if your master strikes you"—he mimes a backhanded blow at Hugo's right cheek—"Hugo, you turn your other cheek. . . ."

Wink is right; he's stuck. He can't backhand the left cheek—it would mean using the left hand. The only other option is a blow, but a blow acknowledges equality. "It really is an act of defiance," he says. "By turning the other cheek, Hugo is saying, 'So what are you going to do now?'"

He asks for another volunteer and explains that in Jesus' time, peasants only had two pieces of clothing, an outer and an inner garment. "In Judaism, the shame fell on the person who witnessed the nakedness," he says, pointing out that when Ham saw Noah naked, it was Ham who was disgraced.

"Jesus says that if they bring you to court, they're going to win. It's their law, they wrote it. So put your creditor in a position where he's shamed: give him your undergarment as well." He stages a CourtTV scene, with himself as the demanding creditor. His enthusiastic victim is down to his underpants before Wink stops him. The audience laughs and applauds, and Wink turns to them, pleased. "You've heard that read in church over and over and never even cracked a smile."

What about the extra mile? "The issue here is *ageria,* the right of a soldier to force a civilian to carry a pack, which he could do—for one mile. What we've failed to look at in this passage is that if he makes you carry it more than one mile, he is in violation of the law." In this skit, Wink takes the part of the victim, waving cheerily at the perplexed soldier who now faces the risk of punishment. "See how much I love you?" Wink gloats happily to him.

"I'm trying to counter the sentimentality with which this passage has been interpreted," Wink says. "George Bush says we've gone the second mile with Hussein, but what he seems to mean is go one mile, then two, then nuke 'em."

Wink asks for other options in dealing with Hussein. What if we chartered the Queen Elizabeth II and went over there for a vacation? he asks. "If you have an armed angel, you don't have an angel that likes vacations."

I'd forgotten about angels. In Wink's mind, all this stuff holds together, but in mine, he seems to be talking about several different things at once: angels, principalities, nonviolent resistance, healing the soul-body split. . . .

The group does its best to come up with alternative solutions, but winds up with more questions than answers. "I'm basically a pacifist," says one woman, "but I have two sons of draft age. Where do we draw the line?"

"Some people would say if we'd applied more violence eight years ago, we wouldn't be here now."

"Getting rid of Hussein wouldn't get rid of the domination system there."

"I'd like to support what we're doing," says one contrarian. "Saddam is hurting his own people, and we need to stop that. We've tried to reason with him, and now we need to go in and get him out."

"It's easier to start a conflict than to get out," Wink responds. "Are you going to go in and fight door-to-door in Baghdad? Even the Pentagon does not want to do that."

"The question is how do we empower the people there to do what needs to be done?" says one woman.

"I'm not sure we can do that," says Wink. "I think we've got to get into a conversation and make an exit strategy for both parties."

"Bush sure got us off to a great start," says a man whose voice drips sarcasm, "calling him another Hitler and not pronouncing his name correctly."

When they come to apply Wink's message to their own lives, though, the discussion gets very interior, very fast. It could hardly be otherwise, as Wink had acknowledged earlier, saying it might be a mistake for this group—himself included—to apply these teachings to themselves. "We are hardly poor and oppressed," he had noted. "But everybody is oppressed by something, and we can all benefit from these techniques."

"My anger is born of pain and hurt," says one woman. "I lose it when I haven't taken care of my own spirituality and run myself into the ground. What's been helpful to me about your message is it's grounded in the spiritual disciplines of the Bible and nurturing Bible study."

"Therapy is helpful," says another. "I've learned to sit back and ask why I'm angry, and maybe just count to ten."

"Something that's very simple and difficult and something we all need to learn how to do is guard our tongues," volunteers a third.

"Think about the epistle of James," Wink replies.

Wink asks them about nonviolence in the community. "Do you know anything about peer mediation in the schools?" About a third of them are familiar with the idea, but it doesn't sound as though there's much of it going on here. But then, the kids in the Myers Park school system are probably reasonably well behaved. He doesn't ask about domestic violence, and I don't imagine they'd tell him about it if he did.

"This is a wonderful moment to be alive and Christian," Wink concludes the session. "I want to encourage you to find ways of going out in this community and training people. We have to be doing the work, not just talking about the idea."

The Bible is important to the people at Myers Park Baptist, Bill Dols had told me. "They take it very seriously. They know in their marrow that this is their book, that what they need to know about God and life is in these pages."

Certainly the Bible is treated with great reverence at Sunday's service: solemnly opened as the procession enters the church, and equally solemnly closed when the ministers and choir leave at the service's end. In between, however, the book is hardly used. The only scripture in the service is a couple of psalm verses used as an introductory prayer, and a short section of Matthew's Gospel read just before Wink's sermon.

Wink gets a lot of pleasure out of elucidating Jesus' hard teachings, and he's chosen another: "Be perfect, as your father in heaven is perfect." That verse caused me a lot of mental anguish, until a priest of my acquaintance told me "perfect" could also be translated "whole."

Wink has another take on it. "Does it help you," he asked, "if I mention that Jesus couldn't have said that, because there was no word in Aramaic for "perfect"? The Hebrews had no concept of perfection, no sculpture or painting of the human figure. When they wanted to decorate the temple, they had to send to Lebanon and Phoenicia."

What Jesus said, Wink tells us, is what Luke has written in his version of the passage: "Be merciful." "God's love is all-inclusive, and the conclusion is that therefore we must be all-inclusive. God's not calling us to something that's impossible; he's just calling us to be good to our neighbors and even to our enemies."

People who teach the Bible generally find themselves talking to the converted. That's who asks them to come and speak, or buys their tapes. But Myers Park was hardly a nest of Wink fans, either before or after the weekend, although he had his admirers.

Ted Lucas, a retired pediatrician, had read part of Wink's trilogy and was grabbed by his explanation of the powers and principalities. "It sort of crystalized things for me," he told me. "I will encounter situations and say, yeah, that's what Wink was talking about. Like yesterday they announced we're going to give this forty-million-dollar bailout to Brazil, and the radio commentator said what is going to happen is the speculators are going to make a killing out of this while the people that need help are not going to get it. I thought, 'This is the domination system.'"

Seeing the Bible through Wink's lens has made his life richer, Lucas said. "I don't feel like I act much differently from the way I have, but I'm a lot more aware, I believe, of what living means than I was. And it does nudge you in the direction of following Jesus. I think his message has been distorted over the years by the church and by the writers of scripture; if you get back to what it's really supposed to be, it's very affirming."

Leta Pittman came to the seminar not for Wink, but for his wife. "I learned to dance and it changed my life," she said. "So when I read about integration of body and mind, I came."

Pittman, who was brought up fundamentalist and describes herself, in Matthew Fox's phrase, as a "recovering Christian," doesn't read the Bible much. "The only book my mother would read was the Bible, and I couldn't see how it was helping her at all. I saw the Bible as an escape from reality for her, and I wasn't going there."

She was especially struck, she told me, by Wink's demonstration of turning the other cheek. "To me that was a different, humorous way of reading the Bible. I'm going through a difficult time right now, and that metaphor had come up. To view it that way was refreshing."

But to Helmut Nielson, Wink offered "another example of how mainline Protestantism is shooting itself in the foot. They're so desperately trying to retranslate biblical literature through gimmicky modern concepts. Inerrancy—which is basically appealing to authority—can be done in different ways, and one of them is to create a screen like feminism or liberation or black theology or the principalities and the powers or the domination system. The Pentecostals and fundamentalists have got it right—you have to get down to what it means to you. It has to get down to the level of your own will, where you're ready to make a decision about it and do it."

Perhaps the most disappointed were the organizers of the event, who didn't get what they had expected. Though he considers himself a liberal, Wink is in many ways closer to the conservatives. Like them, he goes on the assumption that the Bible means what it says. "A lot of people say Oral Roberts is a charlatan," he told me. "But I say if you have complaints about him, why aren't you doing healing services in your own church?"

He and Peter Wagner argue happily about demons. "I said you feel demons jump from on high, and I believe the demonic is caused by an angel turning away from its divine vocation. We had dinner together and really hit it off. Conservatives and evangelicals recognize that I take the Bible even more seriously than they do.

"We are stuck with these texts," Wink told me. "Feminists rail at the Bible and discover the Gnostics aren't all that great either. Are we going to chuck Christianity down the toilet because it's not perfect? That's the point of hermeneutics—to interpret the text in a way that does justice both to it and to the needs of people today."

Wink's appearance at Myers Park had been part of a series called "Jesus at 2000," which had earlier featured Marcus Borg. "I was very disappointed," one member of the planning committee told me. "Our focus was on Jesus, and he didn't speak to Jesus almost at all."

It struck me as an odd remark; Wink had talked about Jesus an awful lot, I thought—and with much more specificity than I'd heard from Borg. But Wink had talked about Jesus' teachings, not about his personality. And he had treated those teachings as instructions. For him, as much as for Billy Graham, the Gospels are a user's manual.

That's not the way the Bible is being taught at Myers Park. For despite its low profile in the church's worship, the Bible is being taught here more extensively than at most liberal churches. Over a dozen small groups are involved in Bible study, Dols had told me.

Dols is the catalyst—Dols and a Bible study series he developed called *The Bible Workbench,* which many of the groups use. The series' approach, Dols told me, "is to step behind the creeds and doctrines and work on the assumption that the text comes to life if you can get theology out of the way. It allows people to engage the biblical text and work out their own salvation through it."

Dols's theory, which comes out of the work of the Guild for Psychological Studies, a California group that tries to link Jesus with Jungian psychology, is that the biblical stories are not primarily theological, or doctrinal, or instructional, but archetypal. "If we put aside for a moment all Christology and start to ask, How am I like Jesus? or How is Jesus like me? it starts to raise the possibility that I might be able to be like Jesus, which is a terrifying thought. It's much more attractive just to worship him."

Wink too was influenced by the Guild for Psychological Studies—that's where he gets his emphasis on movement and sculpture and drawing. But I'm not sure he'd be as eager as Dols to eschew theology.

"The question of the text," Dols says, "isn't, What does it mean? The question is, How is this text happening? How is this story an event in your life?"

As an example of how it works, he told me what he'd done recently in a session on Jesus' warning to his disciples, in chapter 10 of Matthew's Gospel, that they will be hauled before the authorities and persecuted. 'Don't think beforehand about what you will say,' Jesus tells them; 'the Spirit will give you the words you need.'

"We talked about his saying, 'Don't prepare a defense in advance,' and about how we write scripts, and get ourselves ready, for any relationship. Then once we get into it, the other person doesn't have the same script. Why do we do it? What drives us to have to prepare like that? People talked about the need to control, and the fear that we're inadequate, that people don't like us. I had heard a story on National Public Radio about phobias, and they said the top phobia is of standing up in public and making a speech. The theory they were pushing is that the real terror is that we might slip up and tell the truth, reveal what really is there. Then I suggested that there might be a parallel between that and the text, where Jesus is saying that the temple must come down one stone from another. There might be a parallel with the stuff people were saying about rehearsing and stripping. The temple is a metaphor for life. Life is about walls, and boundaries, and turf, and in its center is a box that holds God, with a veil in front of him. The whole thing is meant to protect God and keep people out of center place."

The approach works better with narrative than with explication, Dols said. But because the series is based on the common lectionary, a three-year cycle of Sunday readings used by many churches, he has to deal with all kinds of texts, all of them abstracted from any sense of their context. "We did a passage from Thessalonians last week, which always makes me groan," he said. "I try to use images and metaphors."

I found myself thinking, "But that isn't Bible study" and was embarrassed. When I learned to pray through just this kind of imaginative personalization of biblical texts, it changed my life. And I share Dols's belief that God speaks through even the wildest metaphor scripture can inspire.

But the Bible is not only about what I can extract from it. The Bible was written by people very different from me who had something of their own to say. Recognizing that difference is what helps me remember that God, too, is different from me. If I'm not willing to let the Bible be itself, will I be willing to let God be God? Or will I succumb to the ever-present temptation to turn God into a narcissistic reproduction of my own self-image?

Chapter 5

Winnetka Congregational Church

Winnetka, IL

W hen I found out that Marcus Borg was going to be speaking about the Bible at the Winnetka Congregational Church, I knew I had to go and listen. I grew up in Winnetka. I sang in the Congregational Church youth choir. I taught in its Sunday school—I was even *paid* to teach in its Sunday school, a job about which I had moral qualms, since I was much too shy about religion even to mention God. I hung out with the church's youth group leader and his wife, who wore loose flowing clothes and collected folk art and reeked of urban sophistication.

The one thing I didn't do in the Winnetka Congregational Church was learn anything—anything at all—about the Bible. If it was read in services, as it must have been, it made little impression. What I knew about the Bible, in my teens, I got from reading *The Day Christ Died* and Kazantzakis's *The Last Temptation of Christ.* I didn't get it in church.

Winnetka in the 1950s was as Republican as it was possible to be; not Eisenhower Republican, as my mother (an Adlai Stevenson fan) used to complain, but *Taft* Republican. When Kennedy ran against Nixon in 1960, we held a mock election in high

school. Out of four thousand students, more or less, there were
two who voted for Kennedy—me and my next-door neighbor.

It was a churchgoing town as well, and in that environment, the
Congregational Church served as the church for the non-churchy.
It had no denominational affiliation, no creed, no oppressive reli-
giosity: a Basic American Protestant church with white walls and
straight-backed pews, intelligent sermons, and no demands.

"Did you notice," asked a childhood friend of mine years later,
"that when we joined the church, we never even had to mention
God?" Maybe I hadn't cheated the Sunday school, after all.

I left Winnetka when I went to college, and once my parents
moved to New Mexico, I never went back. After so long a gap, I
was expecting surprises. But the biggest surprise was how little
had changed. True, the community house now sports a well-
equipped health club instead of the tiny movie theater (with children's matinees) of my youth, and the new supermarket a block
away from the church sells liquor. (In the '50s, you had to leave
town to buy booze.)

But the stores that had defined my teenaged rounds—Con-
ney's Drugs, L&A Stationers, the Sweete Shoppe (now renamed
but otherwise identical)—were all there. The shop that sold the
really ugly dresses is still selling them, and they're still ugly. Even
the lingerie store in which I had been fitted for my first bra, by a
martinet who instructed me to bend over and shake my virtually
nonexistent breasts into the cups, is still there. The Congregational Church carillon still rings in the tall white steeple half a
block away from the house where I grew up.

The church, though, has changed. Two of its three pastors are
women. Confirmation involves not the slapdash classes of my
youth, but a year-long process in which Bible reading is required.

The church is blanketed with signs pitching the Borg weekend: a lecture Friday night, an all-day Saturday workshop, and
then the Sunday adult forum—and a sermon, too. It's a Big Deal.
Congregation members have been drafted to ferry Borg back
and forth from the out-of-town motel where he's staying, to
videotape the sessions for later re-viewing, to bring food for Friday's reception and book-signing.

But the weekend does not seem to be a smash hit. The church is only half full for the Friday night lecture—maybe 250 people, many of them from outside the congregation. Attendance on Saturday is even lower—noticeably smaller, Borg tells me, than the 200 or so he usually draws for such events.

From a more forbidding person, Borg's lecture style would seem downright anal. He pulls out a pocket watch, puts it on the lectern next to his papers, and informs us that he will talk for forty-five minutes exactly. And he does. He tells us he will give us the four primary lenses through which he sees Jesus, and he lists them. But all this scheduling and listing is coming from someone who looks like Alec Guinness in one of his less manic roles and who drops regularly into deadpan, dead-on accents. By the end of the weekend, his watch has become another part of the schtick. He has only to pull it out to get a laugh.

"The first lens through which I see Jesus," he says, "is the foundational claim of the discipline of Jesus scholarship itself—that the Gospels are a developing tradition put into written form forty to seventy years after the death of Jesus, and that they contain earlier and later layers of material. The second is the study of ancient Judaism, which emphasizes Jesus' rootedness in his own tradition. The third is an interdisciplinary approach to the study of Jesus, including insights from cultural anthropology, the sociology of new religious movements, and even medical anthropology. And the fourth is studies of religious experience and religious personality types." It's the emphasis he puts on religious experience that makes his own work distinctive—"though what is distinctive," he says with a smile, "is not necessarily good."

His next list is a five-stroke sketch of Jesus. Jesus was a God-intoxicated Jew: a spirit person, a healer, a wisdom teacher, a social prophet, and a movement founder.

Finally, he tells us he's going to give us his one-minute, fifteen-second summary, which he introduces with a story about being totally flummoxed in front of five million people when a television interviewer asked, not the question he'd been told to prepare a minute-and-fifteen-second response to, but a completely different one.

"Well," he says, "that's a four-minute lead-up to a one-minute-fifteen-second summary; and here it is. Jesus was a peasant, which tells us about his social class. He was brilliant—his use of language was poetic and remarkable. He was not ascetic; he was world-affirming—he had a zest for life. He had a social and political passion like Gandhi or Martin Luther King. He was a religious ecstatic, a Jewish mystic for whom God was an experiential reality. He was also a healer. He seems to have been a spiritual presence like St. Francis or the Dalai Lama. He was an ambiguous figure; you could experience him and conclude that he was insane, or eccentric, or a dangerous threat. Or you could conclude he was filled with the spirit of God."

This Jesus, the Jesus of history, did not see himself as the Son of God or the Messiah; he did not talk about himself as the light of the world or the way, the truth, and the life—and that, Borg says, is reassuring. "What would we think of a person who said about himself 'I and the Father are one' or 'Unless you eat my body and drink my blood you shall surely die'? We have categories of psychiatric diagnosis for people who talk like that about themselves."

Those titles come from the community for whom the Jesus of history became the Christ of faith. "The Jewish mystic became the Christian Messiah. As Christians, we are saying that for us, Jesus is the decisive disclosure of God. I'm not saying he's the only one, or even the best—though I'd say he's one of the two best. But essential to the definition of Christian is the confirmation that in Jesus I see the clearest manifestation of what God is like and what a life full of God is like. And tomorrow I will unpack what that means."

The question-and-answer period that follows is, for me, unenlightening; most of the questioners seem to have their own axes to grind. There's a lot of discussion about modern American skepticism, for which Borg places the blame squarely on literalist readings of the Bible. I find the premise of the question almost naive; a country in which 58 percent of the citizens think the teaching of creationism should be required can hardly be described as skeptical.

But as I leave the church, I think about how thrilled I would have been if I'd been offered something like this in my youth. It would have felt like a gust from the intellectual frontier that I so longed to cross. If I had gone, that is; there weren't many teenagers there tonight.

Borg spends a lot of Saturday morning talking, not about Jesus, but about mysticism, about knowing God. He imitates Carl Jung's response to the question of whether he believed in God: "Belief? Such a funny vort. I don't belief in Got—I know Got."

"As an intellectual hypothesis," Borg says, "God is very problematic. If God is not an experiential reality, then there is no reason to take God seriously at all. You might as well be out playing golf."

Jesus' way of wisdom is diametrically opposed to conventional culture, he says. "In conventional culture, we're trying to live up to the culture's standards for the rewards the culture promises for living up to them."

It's also opposed to conventional religion—which, for Borg, is encapsulated by the Lutheran pastor of his childhood, whom he proceeds to act out. "Does God forgive sins?" he asks in a deep voice, shaking his finger so hard his voice trembles and his jowls shake. "It's a perfect image for God as the lawgiver and judge, who sets standards we fail to live up to, although if we repent, they can be taken care of. And all of this is being done because of the promise of heaven and the threat of hell."

Nobody in this church ever promised me heaven, or threatened me with hell. In my childhood, that was left to the Episcopal church. When we first moved to Winnetka, to please my faithful Episcopal grandmother, I went to the Episcopal Sunday school—until one day I came home sobbing in fear after an overeager curate's sermon on sin and hell. The Congregational Church was where you went to get away from that kind of talk.

But when Borg describes conventional culture, this, for me, is the place he is describing. This church felt safe to me as a child not because of any deliberately taught message, but because of the subliminal one: Here is the one place in the universe that you do not have to worry about whether you are being good or not.

Simply by sitting here, you are being good . . . so don't ask the kinds of risky questions that might make sitting here impossible for you. The tradeoff in this place was not heaven instead of hell, but comfort instead of freedom.

Borg is offering freedom. Although he would never put it so grandiosely, he seems to see himself walking in the footsteps of St. Paul, freeing his audiences not from the law of Sinai, but from the law of convention, of rewards and punishments. "The super-ego can be extraordinarily punitive for much of our life," he says. "We live the life of perfectionism, of trying to meet its demands and being hassled by it if we don't. It's the same as Paul's life under the law."

When Jesus talks of dying to oneself, Borg says, he's talking about dying to the world of culture as the center of identity and to oneself as the center of preoccupation. "We in the mainline churches should not let our conservative and fundamentalist brothers and sisters have a monopoly on the language of being born again. It's utterly central to the Christian life."

Though he doesn't tell his audience so, they are getting not just Borg's views on Jesus' message, but a summary of his own spiritual journey. He himself went through just such an experience in his twenties and thirties, he told me—though, being the Lake Wobegon Scandinavian that he is, he said little about it, speaking only of a series of mystical experiences that made God profoundly real to him. "Suddenly I could hear religious texts in new ways." That's where he's trying to take these folks.

Spirituality has gotten a bad rap in the Protestant tradition, he acknowledges. "At Union Seminary in the '60s, spirituality bespoke an inward-turned piety of no earthly good. But in recent years, it's been recovered."

And at the core of spirituality is the sense of a conscious and intentional relationship with God. The key, he says, is intentional. "We are already in a relationship with God whether we know or believe it," he says, quoting Isaiah. "While we were still in our mothers' womb, God knew us."

Listening to the questions, though, I wonder how much of this is taking root. One man wants to pursue something Borg said about Jesus' way being akin to Buddha's. "Buddha says life is an illusion, and Jesus is life-affirming. I don't see any unity."

Borg is dancing on his feet in enjoyment of the intellectual challenge. "But in the Buddhist tradition, when reality is spoken of as nothing with a capital N, it's very much like the Christian godhead."

"You equate experience with relationship," says another man, "and I don't quite get there. To me, they are different."

A third man wants to know where he got his description of what mystics see and feel. "Are there mystics among us?" The idea seems utterly new to him. Yes, there are, says Borg firmly, citing statistics from Andrew Greeley that almost 50 percent of adult Americans have had a mystical experience, and 10 percent have them frequently. If Greeley is right, the odds are that a bunch of people here have had one too. I wonder what they made of it?

After a break, we reconvene for what turns out to be a lecture on the socioeconomics of first-century Palestine. If Wink knew how extensively Borg quotes him—even to the extent of demonstrating his slap-on-the-cheek routine—he might feel more like a member of the club.

Borg is painfully anxious not to scare off his powerful, affluent listeners. "It's not that the elites are bad people. The point is that this is a systemic injustice that's built into the very system itself. When I say Jesus was political, I mean he protested against all this."

He points to Luke's version of the Sermon on the Mount, where Jesus calls the poor blessed. "It's very easy for us as middle- and upper-middle- and maybe even upper-class Christians to spiritualize this, as Matthew has already done, and say, 'Blessed are the poor in spirit.' We're comfortable being hungry in spirit.

"I trust I'm not trying to get us off the hook," he says. But he is—unless he does not realize, as I so vividly do, how wealthy this community is. My parents were, by any realistic standards, rich; almost everyone I grew up with was even richer. If America has an upper class, it lives in towns like this. But Borg is saying that Jesus isn't talking about middle-class folk like them. "Jesus is speaking about the 1 to 2 percent of the people who sit at the top. It's a real different context from ours. And he's not saying riches are bad for the individual. He's indicting the system that shaped things this way."

Jesus' frequent criticism of the temple isn't a criticism of Judaism, Borg goes on. It's a criticism of the ruling elite that ran the temple. "The words Jesus speaks when he cleanses the temple make that explicit. Now we're not completely sure he said those words on that occasion, but Mark reports it, and if Mark's right, it's very striking. 'My father's house was meant to be a house of prayer for all nations, but you have made it a cave of robbers.' He quotes Isaiah and Jeremiah, and he uses it to indict the elites."

It's one the few pieces of textual analysis we've heard from Borg, and now I realize why they're so rare. Hedged with his caveats, the quotation loses half its force. And Borg is a moderate in the field of Jesus studies; he told us earlier that he would put a large proportion of the sayings in every Gospel but John into Jesus' mouth in one form or another. Many of his colleagues in the Jesus Seminar attribute almost all of them to the traditions of the early church. Those *ifs* and *maybes*, though, wreak havoc with the moral authority of the gospel. "The early church says" doesn't carry anywhere near the power of the familiar "Jesus says."

It also explains why so much of this has sounded frustratingly abstract. We are not getting the Bible directly, because Borg cannot give us the Bible directly. The scholarly tests he applies to it are too complex for laypeople even to understand, much less use themselves. Biblical-historical criticism is not an exercise for the amateur. It requires competence not just in Greek and Hebrew, but in a dozen other modern and ancient languages, as well as— as Borg told us yesterday—disciplines ranging from cultural anthropology to economics.

For this intelligent but for the most part biblically illiterate audience, Borg's caveats carry an implicit warning: You cannot trust the words on the page. The thing he is trying to do—to lead us back to the Bible—is the very thing that, by the terms of his own engagement with the book, he cannot do. No wonder he so often sounds more like a preacher than a teacher.

At lunch, I get an object lesson in just how difficult Borg's techniques can be to grasp. The conversation around the table turns to a familiar quote: "I am the way, the truth, and the life. No one comes to the Father except by me."

It's one of the fundamentalists' favorite citations, but it makes this group queasy. It doesn't sound like the Jesus Borg has been talking about. Didn't Jesus know any better? one woman asks. Maybe, volunteers the man next to her, he meant that his death makes it possible for everyone to come to God even if they never hear of Jesus. "Why would he say such a thing?" asks a second woman, almost in despair.

"That's in John's Gospel," I say finally, "and Borg would say if it's in John, he didn't."

The last talk is about the crucifixion and the resurrection, and it is a shocker. Jesus' body was in all likelihood eaten by dogs, Borg says, like the bodies of other victims of Roman crucifixion. The empty tomb is probably an invention of the early church.

This time, he does present his evidence, at least in brief; he has to, when he is tearing apart the deepest Christian myth. The earliest account of the resurrection, from Paul in First Corinthians, contains no mention of an empty tomb, he argues. "Paul lists, in what is presumably a tradition going back to his conversion three years within the death of Jesus, a series of resurrection appearances, and the verb he uses is most commonly used to report visionary experiences. That hunch is more or less confirmed by Paul's including himself in that list, because Paul's experience of the resurrected Jesus was clearly visionary."

I'm skeptical of this argument, because I think it ignores Paul's motives for putting himself in that list. Paul's enemies, of whom he believed himself to have many, are attacking his authority, saying that because he didn't witness the resurrection, he isn't an apostle. And Paul is arguing, as strongly as he can, that he is. If his experience of the resurrection was different from those earlier ones, he is not about to admit it now.

I may well be missing something that would make hay of my argument. But at least I can make it; I can stand up for myself in this debate. I wonder how many of the people sitting in these uncomfortable pews have any resources beyond stubbornness with which to question Borg's conclusions.

Borg is not saying that the resurrection didn't happen; just that it was not, to use his term, a "video-camera kind of happening." It was a visionary event, a new and powerful experience of Jesus' presence. "These are not primarily stories about something that happened one day a long time ago, but about something that happens again and again and again. The central meaning of Easter is that the followers of Jesus continued to experience him after his death, but in a radically new way: no longer as a figure of flesh and blood, confined to time and space, but as a spiritual reality who in their experience had all the qualities of God. Something about that experience led them to call him Lord."

"For me, stories can be true, independent of the history behind them," Borg told me when we met for breakfast the next morning. "I think the difficulty that many modern people have with that, and the difficulty that I used to have, is that modernity, from the Enlightenment up to the present, has identified truthfulness with factuality. There's a great line from Black Elk: 'I don't know if it happened this way or not, but I know this story is true.' Fundamentalists and liberals alike have been infected by fact fundamentalism."

Borg himself didn't shake loose from that fundamentalism easily, he said. He was excited by the historical-critical approach from the moment he met it in seminary. "One element of that excitement was the shift from feeling I was supposed to revere the text whether it made sense or not to the notion that it needs to make sense or it doesn't have to be taken seriously—the shift from the Bible as sacred object to something to be figured out.

Another was the deep and abiding sense I got in childhood that Jesus really matters. When I realized Jesus might have been different from the way he's portrayed in the Gospels, and that it wasn't a settled question at all what he was like, I had a certain amount of passion to try to glimpse this figure who had been so central all my life. And then there was just the derring-do of taking apart something that was sacred—the excitement and almost liberation of watching sacred cows being butchered."

But all this excitement produced vertigo as well. "I can remember taking Old and New Testament, and doing fairly dense reading in one of the big German Hebrew Bible scholars about the patriarchal period, and whether the patriarchs were historical or legendary figures. It included stuff about whether, if they were historical, they were ass nomads rather than camel nomads. And I remember realizing that my whole tradition began with Abraham, who may not have existed, and if he did was an ass nomad, and I felt almost a dizziness, a yawning distance opening between me and the past and me and this text."

I asked him about the conservative argument, most forcefully made by Luke Timothy Johnson, that he and the Jesus Seminar are encouraging people to think that unless Jesus said it, we don't have to pay attention. For Johnson, the word of God comes not through any particular part of the Bible, but through the book as a whole—a point with which Borg does not disagree. Why, then, bother to sort out the historical layers?

"I think some people need to hear that you don't need to take it as historical fact to be able to entertain the possibility that it is true," he said. "There are people who can't hear it if they have to take it literally. There needs to be a certain amount of deconstruction to give them permission to listen."

A couple of months after Borg's appearance, I went back to Winnetka to get some idea of the effect he'd had. The church was running follow-up sessions at which they played and discussed the tapes of Borg's presentations. Half-a-dozen people showed up for the one I visited, and they were Borg fans. "*Meeting Jesus Again for the First Time* was the most exciting book I have read since Jane Austen," declared one woman.

Borg and I had talked about how hard it is to discuss systems of social injustice in a place like Winnetka with any hope of being heard. At one social gathering, he told me, he'd been pinned to the wall by a true dinosaur. "He was anti-immigration and anti-welfare and anti-Clinton, and he didn't even seem to be aware that there might be some cognitive dissonance between how I thought and how he thought.

"The justice talk is the one I puzzle most about," he had told me then. "How to lure people into the possibility that they might see politics differently than typical middle-class folks do. I would love to know how that takes."

Well, the half-dozen people here tonight talk a lot about structures of social injustice—other people's structures. They are fascinated with the social injustices of the ancient Middle East. "That a social reformer could have been regarded as that dangerous," says Cindy in astonishment. "Was it really that repressive?"

"It was not the time and place to be a rebel," says Elizabeth Hopp-Peters, the church's education minister, who is leading the discussion.

"I think that kind of rigidity was pretty much the rule," says Kitty.

"What's interesting for me," says Peter, "is to watch it replicated in Nazi Germany and the Soviet Union under Lenin and Stalin."

"Well, and there are many examples in our current world where there's that kind of a structure," says Kitty. "Think of the tribes in Africa."

"I have a sense that conservative Christians might find a lot of what he had to say about that controversial," says Peter. "And I think they might have trouble with the idea there was a historical reason for his death."

I am annoyed enough at this conservative-bashing to break out of my observer's role. "They're not stupid," I say. "They know there was a historical reason. They just wouldn't think it was the only one."

What troubles this group about what Borg said isn't the politics; it's the issue a friend of mine raised in an argument over whether Mary was really a virgin. "What do you think Luke was doing," he asked me, "lying?"

"Assuming that what Borg was saying was true, were the authors that clever?" asks Cindy. "Were they that brilliant and skilled with words to hide nuggets of meaning that way?"

"I think they were figuring out how to get more people in," says Peter. "Some of the religions growing fastest today provide certainty. There is very little gray. I wonder if the intent when some of these stories were written was to give more certainty. It's more difficult to see complexity and still say, 'I have faith and will believe.'"

"We've got to assume that we are more rich in terms of complex experience and education than they were," Cindy adds.

This is not a group in which the first item on Borg's list of theological interpretations of Jesus' death and resurrection—that it was a sacrifice for sin—goes over big. "It was helpful to understand the historical context for sacrifice," says Peter, "and interesting about how the church twisted that."

"It comes from the assumption that Jesus had to die, and this was the only explanation that made it right," says Hopp-Peters. "You're assuming that Jesus' death was just something that happened—not a political event—and this is how you make good come from it."

"But I don't think God had any control over Jesus' crucifixion," says Kitty, "just as he didn't against the Nazis. How can you possibly love a God who could stop that and didn't?"

"It's a transfer of responsibility," says Evelyn. "If I can give the blame back to God, then I didn't do anything."

"He becomes the Wizard of Oz," says Kitty. "It makes perfect sense, really."

"He put all this in such a way that I thought about it as I had not done ever before, which is always shattering," says Evelyn.

"Especially," Hopp-Peters teases her, "as you've been reading the Bible for years and years."

"Let's not go into that," she responds, smiling.

"Would you agree with Borg that there is more than one way to God?" Hopp-Peters asks.

"I think about the Mormon Church and the various levels of

heaven," says Peter. "I would find that difficult if I were black. How can you have those kinds of assumptions?"

"I cut my teeth on the Southern Baptist idea that this was the only church and you were damned if you were not in it," says Cindy.

"What if you live in a country where there are no Southern Baptists?" asks Peter. "How would you be saved?"

"This church has for a number of years defined itself as not being the Bible Church," said Hopp-Peters when I asked her, the next day, why the people I'd met seemed so much more certain what they didn't believe than what they did. She was talking about *the* Bible Church, a conservative congregation that has aggressively made its presence felt in Winnetka. "Since the Bible Church came to the community, this congregation—which had been fairly biblically illiterate in the first place—has been pushed even further into saying we don't live our lives according to the literal word of God, and furthermore, though it's never even articulated, we might not even want to read the Bible because the fundamentalists are always quoting it."

It's hard to talk anymore about the Bible as the word of God, she said. "The Hebrew word *dabar,* a word, was a powerful thing, with integrity. God would send out a word and it would accomplish what he said it would. God could create the world by words. But in the information age, with words all over the place, for something to be the word of God . . . I think it means something different."

She is hoping, she said, that between the small-group Bible studies the church is beginning to offer and events like the Borg weekend, people in the church will begin to realize that the Bible can be not just exciting and provocative, but ultimately transformative. Interestingly, she seems to regard the small number of biblical conservatives in the parish as a kind of leaven in the lump. "I think the seriousness with which conservative and evangelical Christians approach the Bible and their faith just can't be matched by liberals, and it's too bad. One of the most conservative members of our congregation didn't come to the Borg thing because she feels very definite about the way she interprets the Bible. 'I wouldn't be here today—I wouldn't be alive today—if it weren't for the Bible,' she says. I think people who have had those kinds of experiences need to communicate it somehow to most of the people here who find the Bible a big bore."

She is optimistic. "In the late '70s I was embarrassed to admit that I was attending a Bible study. But nowadays it's out there. I think the Jesus Seminar and the New Age movement are giving liberals permission to be interested in the Bible and faith and spirituality. I think they are going to catch up. They are going to encounter the Bible in different ways from conservatives, but they are going to have a life-changing experience with it."

As I talked to members of the congregation, though, I wondered. Everybody I met insisted the Bible was important. None of them read it. None of them seemed to believe it contained much in the way of truth—either the factual truth the conservatives insist is there, or the deep truth Borg is excavating for.

"The Bible is a fascinating history book—and that's it," said Clarabeth Kerner, a vibrant, elderly woman who has certainly been exposed to it—her husband was a Methodist minister. Indeed, she's given a lot of thought to how the stories of Jesus' miracles could possibly fit into the universe she recognizes. Jesus could have raised someone who seemed to be dead, she conceded. "It's possible to go through a period of not seeming to be alive." But walking on the water still puzzles her.

"I can't imagine doing without the Bible, though I don't pick it up and read it every day," she said. "And I was so afraid that Borg would hurt people's faith. I worry that if we begin to challenge the Bible, we're going to take away the one stabilizing force, which is our faith. But I think he strengthened it. We can stop saying, If this story isn't true, does it mean there is no God? Because he's a scholar and he knows what he's talking about, it's OK for a layman to think that way."

Donna Curry, chair of the church's education committee, has fought hard to get regular Bible study started there. "It feels like it gives our church balance," she told me. "We have this very wonderful group of people, the brightest, just the best human beings—but there was this other part we were missing."

Does she read the Bible? I asked. "I never pick it up and read it," she said. "I don't have any desire to." That's one reason she fought so hard for Bible studies, she explained, and why she attends them. "When you're studying, you're closer to the people you're studying with, and when you're sitting in a room discussing the Bible as a metaphor—of your life, of your friend's life—it absolutely has brought us closer together."

She talks about the parable of the prodigal son. "It becomes all of our families. We all have people in our families who have left, physically or emotionally."

Is the Bible integral to the life of the church? I asked. "It has been one more thing to help glue us as a church community," she said, "but it's not in any way the most important part. It's not, even now, become an integral part—it's only integral in the fact that it's part of half-a-dozen things that are wonderful here."

Kitty Moeller was the only person I talked to who had been at all upset by the Borg weekend, and she insisted that "challenged" was a better word. "I found myself questioning his . . . his certainty that Jesus was no more the son of God than we are."

She smiled ruefully. "That is not an idea that's widely held in our Christian tradition. As he stood in front of us, I remember thinking 'Look, buddy, just because you're a professor . . . You might be wrong.'"

Moeller doesn't know the Bible well either, she says. "I had a child's feeling that this was a sacred book, a special book from earliest times. But as for knowing it intellectually—no. I just knew Jesus was our friend, he was a Christian, he was the son of God."

What role does the Bible play in her life now? "I don't think I could say," she responded. "I see it as a friend and a mentor, but I don't read it. I always know it's there, like a grandmother, if you need it: the Psalms; the Luke story on Christmas eve; the wise men, angel, and shepherds; rolling back the rock at Easter. It's a comfort. It's a knowledge of the stories rather than a literal knowing of the book."

The church staged some seminars before the Borg weekend to get people hyped, and Moeller went to one of them. "One of the men asked whether we would become a post-Borg congregation, and I remember thinking 'whoa.' I think the jury is still out, but I have to say I think the answer will be no. Not everyone even knows it happened. My husband, who's quite involved in the church, only heard Borg's sermon and hasn't a clue what he thinks."

Will there, then, be a post-Borg Moeller? "I'd be interested in studying more," she said. "I think it opened my mind, and I'm happy to have it opened and questioning."

Borg's own faith shone through the weekend, she added. "If he weren't so religious, if he were more intelligent and cooler, and not as loving, I might have been less receptive. It would have been easier to say, 'Sorry, buddy.'"

Borg had given a gift to this church, I thought when I left, but I wasn't sure it was the one he was intending to give. I think he wanted to give them a new appreciation for the Bible he so clearly loves. It's a gift he has certainly given others. Verna Dozier, one of the Episcopal church's most respected and popular Bible teachers, once told me that Borg's book on Jesus had brought him alive for her in an entirely new way. But Dozier already knew the Bible intimately; there was a relationship already there into which she could move more deeply.

To this audience, which hardly knew the book, Borg gave not a way in, but permission to stay the hell out. Over and over, I heard people say how grateful they were to Borg for teaching them that you can discount all or most of the Bible and still be religious. Though they kept telling me how completely they rejected the fundamentalist insistence that they are the only true Christians, they had nonetheless been shaken by it. And why not? When you're not entirely sure what you believe, any statement of absolute certainty is likely to raise at least the whisper of a question: What if that's true?

As much through the sweetness of his personality as through what he actually said, Borg had calmed those fears. But he had not, I thought, brought them much closer to the book to which he has devoted his life.

Chapter 6

Union Theological Seminary

New York, NY

I f you look at the stacks in Butler Library, under 'anthropology of religion,' Christianity is not a religion." Vincent Wimbush, a New Testament professor at Union Theological Seminary and one of its rising stars, is addressing an advanced class on the passion narratives in the Gospels. Right now, he and his students are talking about how difficult it is to connect the Bible as it is academically studied with the Bible of the Christian faith.

"I'm taking a course at Columbia in Asian religion," says a class member with a shaved head. "And when they talk, they talk from a personal position. Scholarly discourse is a part of their piety. But in my experience in the study of Christianity, once a person begins to even suggest that they really believe, or that this has some meaning for them, they are shunned."

"Or to say that the text is relevant to anything going on in the world now," chimes in another class member. "To say this text is relevant to anything other than the ancient world."

Like virtually every other mainstream seminary in America, Union is struggling with an increasing sense of insignificance. To the liberal, intellectual world it so completely inhabits, mainstream religion is dying, if not dead; the congregations into which

84

it sends clergy are shrinking; and if the media want to know what "Christians" think about an issue, they don't turn to Wimbush (or any of his colleagues)—they turn to Jim Dobson or Gary Bauer.

Union's not alone, but it is, perhaps, the place in which this state of affairs carries the heaviest irony. Things used to be so different. A generation ago, when mainstream Christianity was where the action was, Union *was* mainstream Christianity. Its star theologians—people like Reinhold Niebuhr and Paul Tillich—were intellectual household names. Though Niebuhr had died by the time I went to college, one of the things that drew me to Barnard, down the street from Union, was the presence of his widow on its faculty.

To be at the cutting edge of theological study and historical-biblical criticism has been Union's goal ever since its founding in 1836. It *looks* like a seminary, its gothic, vaguely ecclesiastical buildings displaying a solidity that its neighbors, Columbia University and Barnard College, have lost in their helter-skelter building programs.

But Union's elegance is, at this point, mainly on the outside; inside, its declining fortunes are evident in the rabbit warren of dilapidated offices and classrooms that have been squeezed into its corridors. The place is a logistical nightmare; after three weeks there, I still had no idea how to find my way around.

To conservatives, the explanation for the decline of mainstream Protestantism—and its seminaries—is a simple one: they abandoned the straightforward truths of Christianity in favor of intellectual speculation and trendy social and political causes. What surprised me, as I talked to seminary professors and graduates, at Union and elsewhere, was how many of them felt a bit the same.

Not that they're reneging on their predecessors' liberal politics. On the contrary—diversity and radical politics are encouraged and celebrated at Union. An advanced preaching course focuses on womanist and feminist preaching, and ethnic diversity is almost the exclusive focus of its course offerings in church and society. "Does this place have any *normal* seminary courses?" I asked one professor after a couple of weeks, only half in jest.

But for all its radical politics, I also heard—and not just at Union—a pained recognition that in their single-minded striving after intellectual and academic preeminence, institutions like Union more or less abandoned a generation of pastors—and thus abandoned also the congregations that those pastors served. They did not help them teach their people to pray. When he was studying at Union, Marcus Borg told me, there wasn't a single course in spirituality—not surprisingly, given Niebuhr's well-known conviction that mysticism "begins in mist, centers in I, and ends in scism."

Nor did they teach their students to preach. The official liberal seminary line, I was told by an Episcopal priest who once studied and now teaches at one, was that "it was the business of Bible professors to give you the current critical stance on all this stuff, and it was your problem to figure out how you were going to interpret it. They abdicated their responsibility to help their students figure out how to connect what they were learning with preaching and congregational life."

To be fair, students didn't always clamor for such help. Barbara Lundblad, who teaches preaching at Union, told me that during the '70s demand for those courses dried up almost completely. "There was one semester when nobody signed up at all. The students felt that preaching was a hierarchical enterprise and shouldn't even be done."

Wimbush sees traditional biblical-historical criticism in much the same way—as a hierarchical endeavor. Standard biblical exegesis is the exercise of a ruling class, he says, and can thrive only in stable and homogeneous societies like 1950s' America.

"In Germany," he tells his students, "exegesis was training for serving the state. On this side of the Atlantic, with our fake church-state divide, there is a collusion between high church and high society. And Union was a Protestant think tank for that mix of society and culture. We had Union professors going over to Germany to learn it and bring it back."

He is riding what is evidently a hobbyhorse, and his audience is listening eagerly. "We have never had, in my view, an American construal of that whole enterprise," he goes on. "There is no graduate curriculum that takes our setting as its springboard. And I think that explains our irrelevance to society. It's not that what we study is irrelevant—it's explosive. But it's the discourse. If you do it right, you're supposed to have virtually nothing to say to your society."

Another of Wimbush's classes, a graduate seminar, was designed to shift the discourse, not just figuratively, but literally. He sent his students out into the streets of New York to observe the ways the Bible is actually handled in African-American culture. Their topics ranged from biblical typography in the art on display on Martin Luther King Boulevard, to Sister Soulja's biblical rhetoric, to the book's use in a gay African-American church and an addiction treatment center.

Some class members seemed to me, though not to Wimbush, to be stretching it. "There's no visible presence of the Bible at the site," reported a man who was studying the use of the Bible in an African-American dance class. "But the common language between different African-American communities came from the Bible, and it appears whenever and wherever the dancer finds it appropriate."

Another class member expresses some of my skepticism. "But if it's not explicit?"

"Well, it's a broad area," the student replies. "You can go to get a workout, or you can feel like you've been in church."

"Make sure you get particulars," Wimbush warns him. "Once you've fathomed it as deeply as possible and come up for air, you may tell us the Bible isn't there, but I suspicion it is. It's the same for those of you who are studying music. Look for the Bible's embeddedness; the presumption is that it's there."

The Bible is most significant where it is most hidden, Wimbush tells the class. "What makes a culture a culture is that we all agree to forget things, so you want to look for the things that folk have just agreed to forget. One postmodern definition of culture is that it's a kind of collusion to forget."

A lot of their language goes right over my head; these are Ph.D. students, and they've got the sociological jargon down. As I listened to it, I couldn't help wondering how useful their research would be in the parishes into which I assumed at least some of them were planning to go. The first seminaries in this country were more trade schools than scholarly institutions. Now they're a kind of awkward mix, producing high scholarship on the one hand, and on the other, sending students out to work as hospital chaplains in the clinical pastoral education that's become a universal feature of seminary life. I'm watching the scholarly side here; it's not fair, I guess, to demand that it teach pastors their trade as well.

But if biblical studies remain a fundamentally intellectual enterprise, what about preaching? Sermons are, after all, the way most American Christians learn most of what they know about the Bible. How does Union teach students to preach the Bible? To find out, I sat in on an advanced course on preaching as social transformation, taught by Lundblad and James Forbes. Although he no longer teaches full-time at Union (he's now senior pastor of Riverside Church, right down the street), Forbes is another of the seminary's stars. Coming out of this country's rich black preaching tradition, and a famous preacher himself, he helped to spark a new interest in preaching at Union.

It's hard, Lundblat told me, to give preaching students the practice they need—there isn't time to let them preach a full sermon more than once a semester. Instead, to get them up on their feet more often, she asks them for what she calls sermon slices. Today, they've been asked to come up with a story that would make a good sermon opening. Justice Harry Andrew Blackmun had died that week, and one woman tells the story of being taken, as a child, to a peace and justice retreat where she heard him talk about how much he was hated for some of the decisions he had made. The story of Blackmun's growth from conservative to liberal icon moves her almost to tears, but I find my attention wandering. I've already read this, in the obituaries, and I feel as though—as the saying goes—I'm being preached to.

"I thought it was so effective to talk about a person's life and personal transformation and ideals," volunteers one class member, when the story is over.

But another woman asks the same question that was floating around my head: What did this have to do with the Bible? "I guess the story of Blackmun *was* your scripture," she says. "But there are scriptural messages about growth and being open to change."

"Yeah," says the preacher. "There was something I didn't think I really got to, which was that he made constant references to children, and I was trying to make a connection between that and my childlike response to a just person. I could probably find something like that in scripture."

"Sermons that don't connect to scripture literally make me nervous," says another woman. "I know there are various traditions, but speaking from a Christian context, it's harder for me to trust the preacher."

"What is a sermon?" asks one of the men in the class. "Is it defined by being rooted in scripture, or at least in reference to God and the church? And if those things aren't there, what is it?"

"We go weeks and weeks and weeks at the church I go to and don't hear scripture," responds another class member.

"But then what's the difference between a sermon and a lecture, or talk, or meditation?"

Forbes asks them for biblical texts that connect with the Blackmun story, confessing that even he is hard-pressed to think of one. So are they all. One woman brings up Esther, who becomes stronger when challenged. Another suggests one of the kings of Israel, though she can't think of the name. "Not David," she says, in response to the class's guesses. "Not Josiah. A *really* bad one."

Maybe you need a text, not a story, Lundblad says. "You may not want one very strong story alongside another. A story like this might be more powerful in terms of a verse like the first part of Romans—'Do not be conformed but transformed.'"

I have written only two sermons in my life, neither of them brilliant, so I'm no expert. But they're talking about something in which *The Wall Street Journal* trained me well. In journalism, it's called the anecdotal lead. And they're going about it backward. You don't start with the anecdote and then try to find a text—or an article—to which you can attach it. You start by thinking about what it is you want to say. Maybe, I think, it's the unavoidably artificial format of the class that made scripture seem so peripheral today.

The topic next week is "Voices from the Margin," but preaching is almost overshadowed by the political storm in New York over the police shooting of unarmed immigrant Amadou Diallo. Forbes opens the class by talking at length of his reaction. "I have been to more meetings lately about what we are going to do," he says. "A movement is a-making. Concord Baptist is bringing fifteen people to demonstrate every day, and yesterday they were senior citizens. To see ladies with walkers and canes and their hands cuffed behind them . . .

"But speaking of a class in regard to margins," he adds, "I am aware that my tendency to be primarily concerned about Amadou Diallo has left me without much time to be reflective about the four cops. If there is to be significant change, my understanding of where they are coming from is perhaps more important than concentrating on the horrible death of Amadou Diallo. He is dead, but they are alive, and they are legion. Do I understand them?"

"We need to remember," he says a little later, "that the power of transformation is in serious dialogue."

"It frightens me," says one student. "We are about to enter Holy Week, and I am feeling cynical, thinking about the Christ who tried to break down barriers and make the world of those in power inconvenient, and how they took that and crucified it. There is real danger here. He was beat up. How do I create safety in the face of true evil?"

"If anybody is going to be a preacher," Forbes responds wryly, "he needs to have his insurance paid up."

"I am having trouble with the idea that I should love people who hate me," confesses a student who works at an abortion clinic where she faces hate daily. "When people come at me with hate, it's really hard to care where they are coming from."

"As a minister," responds Forbes, "the hardest job for me is to be genuinely loving and empowering of people who are going to use that power to make my life miserable. Martin Luther King and

Jesus Christ messed me up. They keep urging me to do that which is against my biological response, and sometimes I get sick and tired of them. But a religious vocation exposes you to the unnatural, which people in evangelical circles call the supernatural."

She is looking at the floor, frowning. "Does that help?" Forbes asks.

"I have a lot to think about," she says.

Forbes says little, directly, about the Bible, but I am beginning to realize that he is sneaking it in every chance he gets. It seems to me I'm seeing Forbes the pastor as much as I am Forbes the teacher. He is dealing, as I have seen and heard pastors dealing before, with the walking wounded: those who have been so comprehensively beaten up by the Bible, or at least by the way in which it has been represented to them, that its very mention pushes their defenses up.

The discussion of Diallo has left little time for preaching, but towards the end of the class period an intense Englishwoman with short, bleached-blond hair gets a chance. She's preaching about the nativity. Only the voice she wants us to hear is not Mary's, or even that of the baby Jesus, but that of the ox whose manger has been usurped to hold this child. "Domination over animals reinforces the domination of white over black," she says. "Animal abuse encourages child abuse." She cites *Animal Farm* as an example of how animals stand in for oppressed peoples, and *Charlotte's Web* as an illustration of how an oppressed person can make her voice heard.

"That raises a question about whether our biblical call to domination has been subject to misinterpretation," says Forbes, bringing the Bible up again. It may raise the question for him, I think sourly, but not for her. Her authorities are George Orwell and E. B. White.

Why a person who feels beaten up by the Bible would want to go to seminary in the first place bewilders me. But clearly the Bible is not held in affection by many of the people in this class. The challenge seems to be not to explicate the Bible but to escape from it.

Next week, however, there is no escape. The topic is difficult passages, and Lundblad is passing out a list of preachers' nightmares: some of the ugliest stories in the Old Testament, one of Jesus' nastier encounters, and Paul at his most narrow-minded. It feels to me like karma. Dodge the Bible, and look what it spits back at you.

As students begin drifting out, one of them—a Hispanic woman whose heavily accented English I have had trouble understanding—approaches Lundblad, anxiously clutching the list she's just gotten. Does her final sermon have to be on one of these passages?

Oh, no, says Lundblad comfortingly. "Those are difficult texts, for you to do a sermon slice next week. Your final sermon doesn't have to be from one of those. In fact it doesn't have to be from a text at all. It can be from a story."

The woman walks away, reassured. I, on the other hand, storm down Broadway talking to myself like the crazies that used to congregate around the corner of 116th Street and Broadway when I was a student at Barnard. They're giving it away, I fume. They are handing over the Bible to every right-wing literalist who knows exactly what the Bible says and who it excludes. How are liberals to learn to fight back if Union lets its students dodge the book every chance they get? Reading the Bible is not a natural-born skill. If Union doesn't teach people to read it creatively and deeply, guess what? The fundamentalists will win.

They are abandoning this book to the fundamentalists. They are giving up. It makes me crazy.

"I would never say that in an introductory preaching class," Lundblad said to me later when I told her about my reaction. Lundblad, a Lutheran minister, has spent most of her career in parishes. Like Forbes's black-church tradition, hers is deeply biblical.

But, as both of them reminded me, Union's students are not all Christian. "Our pluralistic age has visited on us the recognition that not all religious groups hold the Bible as the central authority," Forbes told me. "We have Jews and Unitarians in that class. But I always insist that preaching has to be a discourse on sacred literature, even if yours is Emerson or Thoreau."

It's true that one of Forbes's roles in that class seems to be pulling people back to scripture when they wander too far afield. I guess I want more. In this place that so often seems embarrassed by the political incorrectnesss of its ultimate text, I want a ringing defense of the Bible's value.

The most popular, by far, of the difficult texts turns out to be the story of Jephtha's daughter, a bleak fairy tale out of the book of Judges. In return for victory in a coming campaign, Jephtha promises to sacrifice to God whoever first comes to greet him when he returns. He is presumably expecting a slave, but instead, his daughter, his only child, comes running out of the door. Jephtha keeps his promise and slays her on the altar.

I wonder whether the appeal of this story is its unfamiliarity—it is virtually never read in churches—or the fact that their way had been smoothed, since one of their reading assignments was a sermon on the passage.

But clearly, the story engaged them. "Jephtha makes this vow himself," notes one woman. "God doesn't tell him to. In fact, God is silent in this story."

"When God is silent, who is the subject of the sermon?" asks another.

The woman who was so uncomfortable with unbiblical sermons says she'd title her sermon "Don't Bargain Away Your Blessings." "Jephtha doesn't trust God," she explains, "and so he bargains away his dearest things. I do that too."

"So you'd preach a pastoral sermon," says Lundblad, sounding a bit disappointed.

It's the stories about women that get their attention; the other popular text is Mark's story of the Syro-Phoenecian woman who asks Jesus for healing for her daughter, only to be compared to a dog. The woman who preached on the ox at the manger says she'd use this story to talk about women on workfare, whose voices we don't want to hear. Nobody mentions the fact that in this text, Jesus does hear—the woman's quick comeback wins his respect, and he does as she asks.

"I want Jesus to apologize for calling her a dog," says another woman. Forbes takes issue with her. If somebody says that homosexuality is a sin, but feeds and takes care of people with AIDS, "they may not be talking justice, but they are doing justice," he says. "We all suffer from pigmentocracy one way or another. I don't care if Giuliani is a racist; I just want him to change his policies."

Lundblad, though, likes the idea. "I'd like to hear a midrash on what happened when a hundred women came to Jesus and demanded an apology for calling the woman a dog."

"What happens," asks another woman, "to people who *don't* ask for what they need?" The demand in this room for a victim is overwhelming; if the story doesn't give them one, they will extrapolate until they find one.

"If Jesus could change, maybe then——" says one of the men in the class.

"You could change," says Lundblad, finishing his sentence. "Not me," he says quickly, "but other people." I think that's a joke, but he's so serious, it's hard to tell.

The energy level in the room seems several degrees higher than it has the last couple of weeks. I'm not sure it's the magic of the Bible; it may simply be that for once, they are all operating out of the same set of references.

But with a few exceptions, like the woman who notices that she, like Jephtha, bargains away what she most values, they are either doing battle with the texts, or using them to attack those with whom they disagree. I am getting a picture of preaching not as the art of listening to a text, but as an act of brute force—wrestling a text to the mat and walking away victorious.

That is not how either Lundblad or Forbes sees it. But then, as Lundblad told me vehemently, the art of preaching is not easily taught. "I am still struggling with the question of what it means to teach somebody to preach," she said. "I come out of a parish setting, and my introductory class is called "Sermon as Meeting Place," to try to get students to begin to think about what it means to have a meeting place between the scripture text and the community text."

Listening to Lundblad, I understood why, in class, she played the peacemaker role, making sure all voices were not just heard, but affirmed. "I ask them to imagine three or four other very specific people hearing this text. What would they find comforting, or aggravating? Pastors do this in a kind of informal way, but I encourage people to begin to do it in a very intentional way, because it's a piece that easily gets lost. People might say this text is a myth, or this text makes me angry, or this text has no meaning to me at all, and they need to let those voices inform their hearing very, very early on."

Students arrive at Union "all over the map" in terms of the Bible, she said. "My sense is that the people here who know the Bible best are the African-American students. They come with a lot of assumptions about certain texts, but they know the stories and characters better than Roman Catholic students, for sure. Unitarians are in another category, because they may not use the Bible as scripture in any way. Presbyterians have to take Bible content exams, so they come in very eager to catch up if they haven't read it a lot. Lutherans get a case study exam where they would be asked to bring in their understanding of the Bible. Episcopal students come in knowing the Bible through lectionary texts. They think of the Bible liturgically—there are Advent texts and Christmas texts."

Whatever I might think of their commitment to the Bible, Lundblad told me the students I'd been watching are dedicated to learning to preach. To get into that class, they'd already had to take a basic preaching class. And none of this was required.

"Students have to take two semesters of Old Testament, and one of New Testament, plus other exegesis courses, and they have to take systematic theology and church history," she explained. "But nothing in the practical field is required except for field study. The chances of a student taking two preaching courses is about one in five hundred."

Lundblad was as interested in my book as I was in her teaching, and as I told her about my travels, she seemed particularly struck by the fact that I was talking to conservatives. "We in the mainline churches have stopped talking about the Bible in some ways," she said. "If the larger culture hears anything at all about historical criticism, it's people saying the Bible doesn't say what you thought it says. We took away all the things that the Bible wasn't, and there wasn't anything left. Now it's hard to say, 'Look at the wonder of this—isn't it great that we have four wonderful resurrection stories?'"

The way the Bible is talked about in the larger culture "feels like somebody is lying about my friend," she said. "I feel like saying you don't know who this person is."

Schools like Union are "utterly removed" from the world of conservative Christians, she continued, in some distress. "It's hard to know how much we should think about that world. We would like to think about being in relation to all kinds of communities, but our primary relationship is to those on the cutting edge. Does that mean that ultimately we end up talking only to ourselves?"

I wanted to talk to Forbes not so much about how to teach preaching, as about the sense I'd gotten that the Bible has been virtually abandoned by the liberals of whom Union is both a symbol and a teacher. His take on it was more complex—not surprisingly, given that he describes himself as an evangelical liberal.

"The key, to me, is the Spirit," he told me. "The same Spirit that engaged the people who helped to give rise to the biblical tradition has to be with the person who reads it, and the same Spirit is also at work in our contemporary, more dialectical approach to biblical interpretations. We believe that the Spirit in our minds helps us to distinguish between the eternal verities at the heart of biblical tradition and what happens to be time-bound. We liberals believe that we are called on in our age to be discerners of what is the core of the Bible's contemporary and continuing meaning. And that's a complex process, not readily available for the sound bite and not so secure that we can say it's bedrock."

At the same time, Forbes said, "we now in liberal circles are right back to the place where, with Sportin' Life, it ain't necessarily so. We not only protect the Bible from elements that would discredit it; we also visit upon other epochs a kind of paternalistic forgiveness for the narrowness of their perspective. Liberals tend to think that their contemporary mind-set is the result of a progressive human maturation of thought, and that the best wisdom is the wisdom of our day."

I brought up the issue of putting the Bible back together—of interpreting it as a story, not as strands. "It is not these truths," he agreed. "It is these stories."

But he took me to task for what he saw as my overemphasis on a particular mode of interpretation. "A person who presents him- or herself before this book, with the Spirit, as one who is trying to forge a connection, can use one word, one line, one paragraph, or even one theme. When there is a longing in the heart, the Spirit is able to use the different genres of this book to do different things for people, and no one category can be relied upon to be the only channel the Spirit is going to use. I'm not going to buy into any reductionisms that say, 'only this way.' Thanks be to God for the way the Bible nourishes conservatives, and hopefully thanks be to God for the way liberals are able to use it as an instrument of liberation.

"Hey," he said, sending me off with what felt like a benediction. "The earth is the Lord's, and this book is the Lord's, and it does duty with all kinds of folk. I don't think you should lock yourself in."

Reconnoitering I

To the reader-response critics I encountered at the Society for Biblical Literature convention, the Bible, or any text, is a lot like a Rorschach test. It doesn't act on the reader; it just reflects back what the reader brings to it. From that perspective, anyone's response to the Bible says a great deal more about the person responding than it does about the book itself. The book, as an independent object, is almost unknowable.

As a writer, my impulse is to reject that theory out of hand. I spend much of my life trying to find the words, and combinations of words, that will carry my thoughts off the page and into the minds of my readers. Writers write—or at least I write—not so much for their own pleasure as to communicate something: facts, ideas, theories, emotions, excitement. My first vivid experience of myself as a writer was not the first time I wrote, or even the first time my work was published. It was the day I saw, sitting across from me in the subway car, a man reading a copy of that day's *Wall Street Journal*. The paper was folded in such a way that the only article he could possibly be reading was one that I had written.

I've been faced, in my career, with enough letters to the editor and angry telephone calls to realize that no, readers don't

always understand what I mean to say—or that, if they do understand it, they are quite capable of refusing, resolutely, to agree
with it.

But I must believe that, for all its misfirings, communication
is possible. If it's not, I'd better find another job.

But as I watched and listened to the way the Bible is read in
the liberal communities I visited, I was shaken. In some way that
I had a hard time getting a handle on, there seemed to be no
there there—or at least no Bible there.

That seems preposterous. Of course the Bible was there.
What else, after all, were all these people talking about?

Well, more and more I came to feel that they were talking
about themselves.

The insight that we project ourselves—our fears and prejudices
and passions—onto people, and texts, around us, was not, of
course, dreamed up by the reader-response theorists. It's a fact of
life, and nowhere does it operate more profoundly than in the arena
of the sacred. The human instinct to make a God in our own image
is a deep and abiding one. And one of the overarching themes of
the Bible is that that is a path that ultimately leads nowhere.

Over the years, I have spent a good deal of time hanging out
with people I loosely describe as spirituality types—people who
take prayer seriously and try to teach others to pray. One of the
most popular authors in this world is the late Anthony De Mello,
who wrote dozens of books suggesting methods through which
readers could use their imaginations to bring them closer to God.
Imagine yourself in the presence of the risen Christ, he suggested in a typical exercise. "Take time out to sense his unconditional love for you as he looks at you *lovingly and humbly.*"

The problem with that approach, for me, anyhow, was that if
I was the one building the imaginative picture, there was no way
I could trust the feelings, when and if they came. There was no
way for me to tell whether they came from God, or from my own
often passionate desire to feel them.

For me, the only trustworthy indication that God is somewhere in my prayer is that it surprises me. If a thought or a feeling makes me jump, makes me ask 'Where did *that* come from?',
makes me gasp in astonishment, then I can at least admit the possibility that God might be at work in it.

Whether we're dealing with God, or another person, or a
book, it seems to me it's that surprise, that moment of aha, that
signals the shift from projecting oneself onto the other to actually encountering the other. Certainly those moments of direct
connection with the Bible had come to everyone I had watched:
Wink and his discovery that angels might be real; Myers and his
epiphany over the Sermon on the Mount; Borg's terrified excitement at the possibilities of scholarship. All of them knew what it
was to hear, and be astonished by, the words on those pages.

But that's not what they were giving their audiences. What the
three scholars—and White and Dols—were offering their listeners were their *takes* on the Bible, each of which, one way or
another, seemed to be several degrees removed from the book
itself. For Myers and Wink, this multifarious book can be accurately viewed only through one narrow lens. For Borg, it is
hedged round with question marks. For White and Dols, it is tol-
erable only when pulled out of any context its authors would recognize. Whatever the Bible was to each of them, none of them
could give the book to us. They could give only themselves—a
gift, often, of great value, but not the one I was looking for.

At the same time that I was listening to liberal readings of the
Bible, I was also hanging around conservative churches, and it
puzzled me that it was the liberals, not the conservatives, who
made me angry. These are my people, I thought; this is my world.
Why is it doing such a good job of pissing me off?

"It's much more attractive to worship Jesus than to follow
him," Dols had said to me when we talked. And his assumption—
that worshiping Jesus (the very thing the Gospels were written to
inspire) was the opposite of following him—was shared by just
about every liberal to whom I spoke.

As far as I'm concerned, it's dead wrong. For me, as for a whole host of immeasurably more holy people ranging from St. Francis of Assisi to Mother Theresa, worshiping Jesus is not just inextricably linked to following him. It's the only reason for attempting it.

This Jesus is not, after all, an easy character; in many ways he's not even very likeable. He makes impossible demands; he can be intolerably rude; and he is insistent that to follow him is to die. During his lifetime, even his disciples made a poor job of it; they misunderstood most of what he said and ran away as soon as it got dangerous.

The Gospel writers acknowledge all this. But for them, writing out of the experience of the resurrection, it's subsumed into a profound experience of the nature of life and the nature of God. The Jesus presented in the four Gospels is like an icon drawn in quicksilver—distant and yet intimate; infinitely various and yet always recognizable, a figure to be either worshiped or ignored.

Instead of this baffling and glorious figure, the people I'd been meeting were offering me a regular guy. Not only that, but a regular guy who looked an awful lot like them; who shared their passions and enthusiasms and in fact had little more than those passions and enthusiasms to offer. And they implied, and sometimes even frankly insisted, that to reject their attenuated Jesus in favor of the far richer Jesus of the Gospels was to go down the path of blind superstition.

Toward the end of my travels, I went up to Cambridge to talk to Peter Gomes about the biblical hole I'd felt in the center of the liberal churches I'd visited. "It's very hard to warm hearts with a documentary hypothesis," he said to me, hitting the nail on the head. "They are preaching the recipe, not serving the meal."

Chapter 7

Woodmen Valley Chapel

Colorado Springs, CO

C olorado Springs hangs between two worlds. To the east, sloping down to the edge of vision and beyond, lie the Great Plains. Out of the hills to the west rise the snow-covered peaks of the Rampart Range, with Pikes Peak looming above them.

It is a town divided, not just geographically, but psychically. In the last couple of decades, Colorado Springs has been either cursed or blessed, depending on your point of view, by the arrival of close to a hundred conservative Christian organizations. The Navigators, the International Bible Society, Every Home for Christ, Promise Keepers and, most notably, Focus on the Family, have all set up shop in Colorado Springs.

They have met, for the most part, a warm welcome. As a military town (it's home to Fort Carson and the Air Force Academy), the Springs has always had a substantial conservative contingent. Now that it has become a mecca for the religious Right, that contingent is growing by leaps and bounds. New housing developments are pushing the town steadily eastward, and the people who move into them are flocking to the new conservative churches that have opened up all over town.

But back in the foothills, where the town began, there is less

joy. Many of the Springs's long-time residents, faithful churchgoers among them, resent being forced to live in what the
conservatives call a "Christian" town; they know that the word
Christian, used as the conservatives use it, does not include them.

Jann Heinmetz, an official with Campus Crusade for Christ,
serves as the unofficial director of a coalition of conservative
churches called the Net. He told me that the organization wel-
comes any church that accepts its basic principles. To make their
participation easier, it even avoids conservative buzzwords like
"inerrant" and "infallible" when talking about the Bible. "We're
not a bunch of ultraconservative, right-wing Republicans, whatever people think."

But he also, throughout our conversation, described the
churches in the Net as "life-giving."

"What are the rest of the churches in the Springs, death-
giving?" I finally asked. He grinned uncomfortably. "Our emphasis is in giving life, not in doctrine or tradition or liturgy," he said.
"We're not implying other churches are not life-giving."

The other churches, though, don't see it that way. To them,
the conservatives are an occupying horde that has taken over
their town and has no use for them.

The relationship is not so much one of enmity as of absolute
separation. Conservative Christians, feeling as they do that
American culture has turned away from God, tend in any event
to feel safer in a Christian cocoon. When the Net surveyed the
members of its participating churches a year or so ago, it found
that more than three-quarters of them limit their social contacts
either entirely or primarily to other Christians.

But then, in Colorado Springs there's no *need* for relationships
outside the church. You can wake up to Christian radio after a
good night's sleep on a mattress you bought at a Christian bed-
ding outlet; pick up the car you're having fixed at a Christian
automotive shop and drive out to check on the new house the
Christian contractor is building for you—on property you bought
through a Christian Realtor. You can study the Bible with other
Christians on your lunch hour, and on your way home, drop

papers off with your Christian accountant, pick up a book from the Christian bookstore, take a class in Praise Aerobics, and get your hair done at the Christian salon. On the weekend (when you're not in church), you can climb mountains—and pray at the top of them—with other Christians. There's even a Christian Four-Wheelers Club.

But if the conservatives live in their own world, so do the liberals. In the Bible studies I'd attended at the liberal First Congregational Church downtown, I was stunned to hear one member declare that in the twentieth century, people find it hard to take the Bible seriously. "It's viewed as literature, relevant only in its historical context, and not as inspired or religious." He was, of course, right—about the world of which he considers himself a citizen. But in the world where he actually lives, fundamentalist billboards line the roads and churches compete on just how Bible-believing it's possible to be.

It's easy to see why the two camps don't communicate. Some 96 percent of those who go to Net churches believe the Bible is accurate in all that it teaches, and 93 percent believe only those who have accepted Jesus will go to heaven. Three-quarters of them spend time praying and reading the Bible at least twice a week; half of them do so daily.

The responses of the folk at First Congregational to their survey revealed a starkly opposing view. None of them believed that only Christians go to heaven; only two (of ten) use the Bible to help them make decisions; and though most of them pray at least weekly, almost none of them reads the Bible more often than once a month. Half of them only pick it up once a year.

As I poked around town, though, I found some breaches in the walls. For instance, the town won national notoriety in 1992, when Springs-based Colorado for Family Values—backed, it seemed, by every conservative church and parachurch organization in town—sponsored Amendment Two to the state constitution, specifically denying the protections of equal-rights laws to homosexuals. The amendment passed by a 53-percent majority and would be in effect if it had not been struck down as unconstitutional by the Supreme Court.

Surprisingly, the conservatives I spoke to seemed relieved by the court's decision. Their churches, I was told several times, no longer support the amendment. "It hurt us," Heinmetz told me. "That's not the way we are, but even my neighbors think, 'you are the guys that hate homosexuals.' We're known for what we hate. That hurts deeply."

Though most conservative Christians in the Springs seem to hold Focus on the Family in high regard (at least judging by the slight tone of reverence with which anybody who works there was introduced to me), I picked up a strong undercurrent of resentment. "As a father," Heinmetz told me, "if my son was to get involved with drugs or get a girl pregnant, I don't want to know about the depravity of Washington D.C. or the horrendous things the Democratic Party is doing. All I want to know is what I can do." I heard from conservatives as often as from liberals that right-wing Christian "spokesmen" didn't speak for them.

Ministers of liberal and conservative churches do meet together occasionally, though the discussions are sometimes tense. But some unlikely friendships have developed as well; the head of the Colorado Springs Association of Evangelicals told me that he regularly lunches with the lesbian pastor of the local Metropolitan Community Church. (They take care, though, to choose restaurants where they're unlikely to run into members of either of their churches.)

To my gay friends in New York City, Colorado Springs is enemy territory. Reports from my sister, a member of First Congregational who has lived in Colorado Springs, off and on, for over thirty years, only reinforced that impression. Throw in her comfortable guest room, and the Springs seemed like a good place to find out how conservative Christians read the Bible.

In the parking lot of what looks like a shopping mall, a small crowd is admiring a shiny new red convertible. But these folk aren't shopping; the shops have been converted into classrooms, and they're waiting for Bible study to begin.

In the session on First Peter I'm headed for, there's a question written on the dry-erase board at the front of the room.

"When you strip furniture, what method do you use?" But the writer had second thoughts; "when" is crossed out, and "if" is written above it in bright red.

Jim Tomberlin, pastor of Woodmen Valley Chapel, had urged me to visit any Bible studies that struck my fancy. He and his church make a profession of being welcoming. They call themselves, in what has become an evangelical cliché, "seeker-friendly." The very name, Woodmen Valley Chapel, sounds like something Bing Crosby might have sung about when he wasn't dreaming of a white Christmas: a pine-log building in a forest clearing, with windows looking out onto the mountains and birds singing in the trees.

But when you turn right on Woodmen Road as it splits from Rockrimmon, you find not rural coziness, but huge parking lots and modern buildings of glass, rock, and wood, with Ponderosa pines scattered around the grounds to give at least a faint air of rusticity. It's an example of that increasingly prevalent suburban institution, the megachurch. Woodmen Valley started twenty years ago in a converted chinchilla house. It has since outgrown three buildings, and eight years ago took over a nearby mall, a couple of blocks from its main campus, to handle the overflow.

Four thousand people attend the three services that begin Saturday evening and continue into Sunday. The main sanctuary resembles a plush high-school auditorium; rows of cushioned seats sweep upward from a stage that's flanked by projection screens. There are none of the traditional church props: no cross, no robes, no hymnals, no flowers. What goes on here looks more like a camp meeting than a traditional Protestant service. There's no choir, no processional, not even any Bible readings. Instead, a musical group sings soft-pop Jesus songs while Tomberlin, a yuppie-ish, friendly looking man in a blue shirt and khaki pants, walks the aisles like Bill Clinton working an audience.

It's all very laid back—until, after the singing and the prayers for mothers (it's Mother's Day), Tomberlin starts preaching.

"There're three views about human nature," he says. "Some people think it's good, but with a tendency toward evil. Some people think it's evil, but with a tendency towards good. But the Bible's view is that it is bad—and with a tendency toward evil."

Just to make sure we get the point, he gives us the name for the doctrine he's preaching: total depravity. "It's not PC," he says, "it's not popular. But I'm going to prove it to you; we don't teach children to lie, but they do."

The good news, Tomberlin says, is that this "sin nature" has been destroyed by Jesus on the cross. As a result of his sacrifice, it is now possible for Christians (and only for Christians) to live what he calls an exchanged life. Most of us don't believe that, he says. We are like dogs conditioned by a buried electrical fence; even though the power of sin has been turned off in our lives, we act as if it's still there.

His sermon—disorienting enough in its combination of laid-back friendliness and fearsome doctrine—is equally mixed intellectually. He's telling jokes with a Greek lexicon in his hand. In one breath he gives the subtleties of the Greek word *logizomi* — it means "count on" in the sense that an accountant would use it. "It's a CPA term," says Tomberlin.

A couple of minutes later, he's going for laughs with a long story about a woman who stole his parking space, and how much he wanted to let the air out of her tires.

Christians are the only ones, he says, with the authority and power to say no to habits and addictions. "So when your anger reaches the boiling point or you want to reach for the second piece of pie, or a drink, or a drug, or a porno magazine, you don't have to answer when temptation comes knocking at your door. That old man doesn't live here anymore. Just say Jesus, would you mind getting that door?"

There's a collection and another song, and it's over.

Used as I am to an elaborate (and lengthy) liturgy, I left Woodmen Valley wondering how, if that's all there is to it, the place draws such crowds. Megachurches are often accused of appealing through a kind of Christianity Lite, but you could hardly make that charge against Tomberlin's theology. His doctrine is heavy enough, but where was the sense of community, the chance for intimate friendship, that for me lies at the heart of a lively church? Nobody even invited me to coffee hour.

There's community aplenty in megachurches, I was to discover. Not in the service, but in the small groups that make up the inner life of these huge organizations. These groups, containing anywhere from six to a couple of dozen people, meet weekly for prayer and Bible study, often right before or after a service. These are suburban families, and overscheduled: they juggle Little League and chores and work they've brought home, and they're not going to spend all day Sunday and maybe a weeknight or two at church the way their grandparents did. So Woodmen Valley makes church convenient. It offers Saturday night services, a coffee bar, brunch for people with time to kill before they pick up their kids or go to their own small-group meeting, and traffic cops to speed them home afterwards.

Woodmen Valley is growing some 30 percent a year, and it doesn't have time to give small-group leaders a lot of training in how to teach the Bible, Tomberlin told me. Indeed, he himself isn't big on formal theological training; though he has a seminary degree (from Dallas Theological Seminary), he's the only one on his staff who does.

Chris Baumann, who leads the first group I visited, and who posed the question about stripping furniture, taught himself to teach. He takes it seriously; he spends four to six hours a week preparing for the class, he told me, using a variety of commentaries and praying over the passage.

Stripping paint is a metaphor for the Christian life, Baumann tells his class, once they've exhausted their paint-removal techniques. (It doesn't take long—their answers to his question range from "Let someone else do it for me" to "Sell it" to "Burn it" to "Hire a stripper and watch her do it.") As new Christians, he explains, we come out all bright and shiny, but then we start getting scratched, and adding layers of paint. God, the furniture restorer, puts us through pain and difficulty to bring us back to our shiny selves.

The class picks up the metaphor with the ease of long practice. "When we were putting a lot of pain and effort into a rocking chair," says Terry, "I was thinking about God putting time and effort into me."

"You have to use tools," chimes in her husband, "and maybe

things that happen to me that I don't like are tools that God has put together."

Baumann points them to chapter 2. "Rid yourselves," he reads. "In Greek the term has the meaning of being repentant. Strip yourself; get back to the new clean Christian that you can be and allow God to help you along the way. If you have paint on to cover the ugliness in your life, how are you going to love your brother?"

"But you're assuming," responds Terry, who seems to share Tomberlin's view, "that the furniture's good to start with. We don't come that way."

"No, the wood is good," argues Ed, a white-haired man who'd introduced himself to me as a recent arrival from California. "That's why you're going to strip it. God didn't make junk when he made us."

They are pushing the metaphor hard: Jesus chose all kinds of strange characters for his disciples, and stripped them down. The most difficult layer to get off is the first one, that our parents put on.

Baumann tries to pull them back to the text, but gets stuck in his own gimmick. "Look at Peter," he says, reading verse 2: "'Like a newborn baby craving pure spiritual milk.' That's a very important verse for me. God wants us to grow up and be Christ-like, but we need to be fed, we need to do spiritual work, so we don't require coats of paint."

You can stay clean, he says, citing antique furniture. "The owners took good care of it."

"They didn't have kids," comes a sour interjection.

"It's possible," Baumann argues, "to have the beautiful and glorious God-given state all bright and shiny, but it takes work."

Baumann uses metaphors and analogies to make biblical teaching relevant to his students' lives, he told me, when we met for lunch a few days later at a beer and hamburger joint on Colorado Springs' main shopping street. "One of the worst things I have ever gone through is a Bible study that's so academic it has no relationship to how you live," he said. "The reason we have as much fun as we do is that we try to relate it all back to each other."

He also likes to shake up group members' thinking. "When we did a session on teenagers, one thing we used was a passage out of Deuteronomy that says, 'Teach a child his ways and he will remain with the Lord.' The question was how much strictness and discipline to give them and how much freedom, and I took the tack that God wanted everybody to be superstrict. All of a sudden people in the class started saying you have to let them make their own choices. I will often play the devil's advocate."

The people in his class look to the Bible as a guide to behavior, he said, but it's not a clear-cut set of rules. "Jesus spoke in parables," he said. "He gave analogs, as opposed to directives or commands. There are a few simple prescriptions—the Ten Commandments, the great commandment to preach to all nations—but everything else demands a decision by the individual about how they're going to walk the path of God. It's one of the hardest things you can do."

I mentioned the expensive new car outside his classroom. "Jesus talks often about how the hardest thing is for a rich man to be a Christian," he responded. "Wealth is a problem. But is it a sin? It depends on how you act on it."

Money is certainly an issue at Woodmen Valley. Tomberlin himself is on a fierce campaign against indebtedness, refusing to allow the church to borrow money even for new buildings, and telling members it's a sin to pay interest on credit cards.

It all comes from the Bible, Tomberlin told me, citing Malachi 3 on the principle of tithing and First Timothy on being content with what you have. "We believe God's word here," he said, "and God says if you give me a tithe, I will take care of you. So if at the end of three months God hasn't taken care of you, we will give the money back." Only one person has taken him up on the promise, he said.

Baumann described himself to me as a libertarian whose only economic concern is earning enough to support his family. But he's an eager supporter of tax limits. I asked where he finds tax limits discussed in the Bible. "Scripture doesn't say anything about that directly," he conceded, "but indirectly I think it says a good deal." But the texts he came up with—Jesus' injunction to give Caesar what is Caesar's and Paul's to support the local authorities—didn't seem to prove his point, forcing him to back-track. That's good advice in general, he said. "But the problem you run into is if individuals get into office that don't have God in their heart."

That got us onto politics, a vexed issue among Colorado Springs churchgoers because of their bitter experience with Amendment Two. "You cannot use the Bible as a political guide," Baumann said flatly. "Politics are driven by the social fabric of individuals that make up the community." But, he added, the people who make up the community, at least the Christians among them, are shaped by their understanding of what the Bible demands.

"If you acknowledge Jesus as Lord in your life, then it doesn't matter how dirty or ugly you were before," he said. "But there's a passage in Colossians about not allowing the rules of men to bend the law of God. I apply that to a lot of things. When I make a decision about moral values, I will look at what the Bible says in its entirety and then ask can I live with this situation or do I say it's wrong?"

For example, he said, "I'm very against abortion, but the Bible tells us strongly, you're not to judge. If a person does abortions or gets one, that's between them and God. It's not my business. But if the government does something to the family, where I have responsibility, that is my business."

A few days later I come back to the strip mall for another Bible study, this one on the book of Acts, Luke's romantic picture of the early church. This is a more laid-back crowd than Baumann's group. The leader is sitting on the teacher's desk, strumming a guitar. Whoever brought chips and salsa forgot the plates, so people are balancing their chips on coffee filters and dipping the salsa out of paper cups. They're talking about real estate. One couple is moving out of state and needs to borrow a truck, and their next-door neighbors, also in the group, are worried about who's going to move in.

Dean, the leader of this group, asks for prayer requests and praise reports, which produces what, in another context, would be a casual exchange of news. Evelyn has begun writing theme letters to her son in the marines; Kathy has decided to become a foster parent, and has spent the day buying baby furniture at garage sales. Jerry, a software developer, is feeling stressed out as launch date for a new program looms closer. There is thanksgiving for the success of a daughter's sleep-over party the night before, and a prayer, in the midst of extensive dental work, for help in witnessing to the dentist. Pat and Dan, next-door neighbors to Dean and his wife, are moving; Dean is hoping the new buyers are seeking God.

Like Baumann, Dean starts with a question, though one that has more obvious relevance to the subject at hand. "What do people go to church looking for?"

Coffee and donuts. A mate. Chips and salsa.

But gradually the discussion takes on a more serious tone. "I go to feed at the trough," says Dan. "And sometimes," Pat chimes in, "we get salad with no dressing, and sometimes we are just astonished."

They know—physically, at any rate—what they want out of church: a place to park, a comfortable seat, air-conditioning, a short service. "We went to a black Southern Baptist church," says one woman. "A three-and-a-half hour service, and then lunch afterwards. We were dying."

"As I prayerfully considered the lesson, it seemed to me it was talking about church," says Dean. "It's the very first use of *ecclesia* in the Greek, which means 'called-out ones.' A congregation once restricted to the congregation of Israel now includes all of Jesus' followers. What attracted them?"

But the discussion that follows very quickly shifts from the appeal of the early Christian church to church life today. Some believed, says Dean, and some were merely curious. Who are those people now?

They visit regularly but don't sign on, says Jerry. They don't want to be asked to change.

"People like that probably more often go to a less-challenging church, a more dead church, a church that won't ask them to change," adds Dean's wife. That starts them on a litany of other churches' failings: thinking Jesus is one of many ways to God; validating any lifestyle even if it's against what the Bible says; offering predictable services; not touching the heart.

"I've heard it quoted," says Kathy, "that 55 percent of the people in a Protestant church on any given Sunday have never given their lives to Jesus Christ. I don't know if it's true, but even if it's just a portion of that, there is a tremendous mission field around us."

"And at work," adds her husband, telling them how, during his weekly lunch with a friend at Denny's, they've become acquainted with one of the waitresses. "She's a single mom and works two jobs, and she talks about the good and bad things in her life. I just recently got to the point of asking her about her faith, where she is in her spiritual journey, and she talked about the Catholic Church and how she needs to go more." Afterwards, he tells them, he and his friend realized "that there among us is someone who never gave her life to Jesus Christ. We're praying that maybe the Lord will use us to help her know Jesus."

"In the light of this passage from Acts and other Bible verses," asks Dean, "what does Jesus want his church to be and do in the world?"

"For me, it's Matthew 25," says Kathy, who'd prayed about her fostering plans. "I guess that's how I see my walk in life, to be willing and ready to give a cup of water. To a degree, fostering is along those lines. I get a lot of criticism from people who ask how I can take care of this baby and then give it up. But the baby's going to be here anyway, so why can't I be involved?" She had been hesitant, she says, to work through a government agency instead of a Christian one. "The pastor was bugging us to get out in the world, but I was holding back. But it's stupid to know I have this gift, which I know isn't all that prevalent in the world, and not use it."

All of them, it seems, have either feared venturing away from the Christian cocoon or been criticized for doing so. "It took me awhile to get over my prejudice against working for the government," says Dan.

Dean says one of his pet peeves is when Christians criticize other Christians for stepping outside of the Christian world.

"People are very quick to criticize a musician who plays for a secular audience, and it blows my mind. Everyone complains about
how cruddy the airwaves are, but as soon as a Christian takes a
step in that direction, it's 'Oh, what are you doing?'"

"You have to get out in the world and do what you're supposed
to do," says Jerry. "I work for a company that makes a whole lot
of people rich, and most of them are not Christian, but that's
where God put me. People think there is a Christian cage you're
not supposed to step out of."

"That's right," says Dean, waggling his finger in imitation.
"'Get back in the box. No, no, no.'"

There are stories about this problem in Acts, and all through
the Christian scriptures; it was one the early church faced over
and over. But that's not where, in their passionate wrestling,
these people are turning. They are citing something vaguer—a
mutually accepted amalgam of teaching, culture, and instinct
that they call biblical faith. It's a way of looking at the world and
the reality of God that's firmly buttressed by concepts drawn
from the Bible, but which does not seem to be, at least in this discussion, the result of a direct encounter with it.

In one way, that's not surprising. If the question I want answered
is, What should I do, right now, faced with this twentieth-century
problem? the Bible is probably not the easiest place to find an
answer. It is, as Baumann said, too indirect.

But these are people who believe the Bible *is* the book with the
answers, and it seems to escape their notice that they're not actually turning to it. Instead, they're recycling words and phrases from
the Bible, mediating and clarifying their meaning through discussions like the one they're having now, until each one becomes the
trigger for a whole repertoire of behavioral expectations.

"We are to be a light in a dark world," says Dean, running
through a litany of touchstone phrases. "We are to be in the
world and not of it, to be salt and light, and to some we are the
smell of death, but to others we are the smell of hope."

And the behavior these phrases trigger? "I go down to the Y

and play racquetball and make friends," says Dan, "and I hope I spread light. People say they like to play with me because I don't lose my temper. I ask folks 'Do you attend church around here?' Or I say 'When did you become a Christian? Tell me about that.'"

"We shouldn't judge," says his wife. "When you go to the store and see a mom who's like 'I said get away from that, I'm going to spank you,' it's better to say something sympathetic or try to distract her. To help her out instead of judging her."

"You have to step out of your comfort zone and listen to the Holy Spirit," says Kathy.

"Jesus wept for people," says Dean. "He knew their issues, and he had compassion for them. He didn't come to condemn the world, but to save the world, and we have the same mission statement as he did, to seek and save the lost."

Our time is up. "Praise the Lord," Dean says in dismissal. "Go and lend trucks to one another, and encourage one another."

"I believe and teach that the Bible is our operator manual," Tomberlin told me when we talked in his office, rich with books and dark wood. "It's user-friendly soul food."

Like most of the people I met in Colorado Springs, Tomberlin does not believe in strict biblical inerrancy—the doctrine that every word in the Bible is factually accurate. "Jesus spoke in Aramaic, but the writers wrote in Greek, and I realize that things get lost in translation, which is why we need to get back to the original words."

But he comes pretty close. "When God spoke," he said, voicing a common concept in evangelical faith, "he didn't stutter."

Some of the people I'd met in Colorado Springs described Tomberlin as shallow, and I could see why. He didn't seem so much to think before speaking as to dredge up the appropriate response from some interior tape library.

"A lot of people think if you don't yell at people, if they're not condemned or slapped around from the pulpit, they haven't been preached to. Well, if the gospel offends them, so be it. But not my tone of voice, or that I'm speaking Christianese. I don't use 'born again' or 'washed in the blood'; I try to use language that a person who has never been in church would understand. I believe the Bible is more relevant than today's news. When people come to our church, we want to create an environment where they feel safe to invite neighbors and coworkers who aren't churchgoers. We're not going to come off like right-wing extremists. We're going to love them"—he grinned—"and serve them cappuccino."

Tomberlin leads the church's small group for brand-new Christians. One question he often gets is, "How do I know this is the word of God?"

"Well, that's a very honest question, so I say let's delve into it. What is the evidence we can trust? There are the self-statements—but that's circular reasoning. What about the history, how it was put together, how its teachings have changed people's lives? There is a science of textual criticism; Jesus quoted from every book in the Old Testament. This gives credibility."

Though I suspect we mean very different things by the phrase, I share Tomberlin's belief that the Bible is the word of God. But listening to him defend that position, I found myself silently tearing his arguments into shreds.

Even for Tomberlin, it turned out, they weren't the point. "People who ask this question aren't asking it from an intellectual point of view. They're asking can I rely on this? Does this work in my life? They want to have a God experience.

"They have given up on church," he said, smug as a salesman who's got the market cornered. "80 percent of the churches in America are dead or dying. They may be orthodox or nonorthodox, but they're not meeting the felt needs—or the real needs—of people. There's nothing happening, and they ought to close their doors."

As Tomberlin poured out one well-rehearsed speech after another, I felt less and less as though I was learning anything. People want mystery, he told me; they want instruction; they want answers; they want to be comfortable; they want a relationship with God; they want to be loved. Right. Jim White gave me the same list; so could any pastor in the country. Tell me something I don't know.

As I was about to go, Tomberlin started talking about a recent sermon about Jacob, who wrestled all night with God. "You may think that your problem is your boss or your spouse," Tomberlin had told his congregation. "But until you do business with God, you can't do business with your past. Jacob's character is described in his name, the heel-grabber. He's a manipulator, a conniver, and God said, 'I can't use him till I have a character adjustment here.' God touched him at the point of his greatest pride and broke him.

"What people need is to be told that there is meaning in what they are going through," Tomberlin said to me, "and to be told that from the Bible gives them a great ability to hold on. The Bible is God's heart, the story of God's love for us, and people need to hear that God loves them. They flock to churches that will teach that."

What made it so hard to get a grip on the Bible from Tomberlin, I began to realize, was the same thing that made it hard to get a grip on it at the Bible studies I'd attended. Both distilled the Bible into talismanic phrases rich with the promise that encounter with God is possible. But both ignored—in fact, denied—the crotchety richness that, for me, makes the Bible a place where that encounter happens.

Chapter 8

New Life Church

Colorado Springs, CO

Y ou've really got to talk to Ted Haggard," said almost everyone I met in Colorado Springs. And all with exactly the
same expression: an amused and quizzical anticipation.

Haggard is founder and pastor of New Life, the biggest
church in town, and a prominent character in the Springs—a
poster boy for the Christian Right. Bill Moyers spent a lot of time
with him when he came to town, and so did the makers of
another PBS special, *Affluenza.*

"Oh, right," I said to him when I finally figured out that's
where I'd seen him before. "You were the guy at the picnic
table."

"With the goat," he said.

But meeting Haggard was easier said than done. He couldn't
do Monday—he saved Mondays for his family. Tuesday,
Wednesday, and Thursday he would be praying and fasting. "I
know," he finally said. "This'll be fun. I'm going to miss the main
service this Sunday because I'm going to go to a black Pentecostal church to wash the pastor's feet. I'll bet you've never seen
that before. You come to the early service, and then go with me.
We can talk in the car."

This was more of Ted Haggard than I had planned on seeing,

119

and my uneasiness only grew when spread all over three pages of Sunday morning's *Colorado Springs Gazette* was a story about another of Haggard's activities: the World Prayer Center. It was, the paper said, a twenty-four-hour-a-day, high-tech, Internet-linked command center for an international prayer campaign to spread Christ's message to the unconverted. Peter Wagner, a prominent evangelical, was quoted comparing it to NORAD, the military command center buried deep under Colorado Springs. The prayer center, he said, would be "the most powerful air force in the invisible world." Haggard told the paper he got the idea in a vision, in a pup tent on Pikes Peak.

The NORAD of prayer? Visions? Washing feet? As I drove up Academy Road, past the headquarters of Focus on the Family, I wondered nervously just what I had let myself in for.

Haggard, a hyperactive blond with a smile so enormous you expect the rest of his face to fade away like the Cheshire cat's, took me on a rush tour before the 8:30 A.M. service. The place was jumping, even at that hour. The Sunday school rooms looked like something out of Disneyland. Fort Victory, a cowboy town, included a trading post (the kids get wooden nickels for attendance and achievement, and can trade them for prizes); younger kids get a Caribbean seaside town and a Sesame Street–type playground. Haggard's route through the main hall was punctuated by hugs and high fives, but he paused long enough to grab a book out of the bookstall and hand it to me.

Jazzy music came out of the main sanctuary. Like Woodmen Valley's, New Life's sanctuary looks like an auditorium, but lightened by a greenery-filled stage. Haggard's seat, in the front row, is equipped with a telephone. He swore to me that he has been known to cancel the service and call out for pizza.

As the singers jumped up and down on the stage, people in the auditorium swayed back and forth, arms lifted. I quickly learned why reporters—even liberal ones—like Haggard; as the service proceeded, he kept leaning over to fill me in on the background of what I was watching. "This guy who's the worship leader," he told me at one point, "I met him when he was a senior in college.

He was so depressed he locked himself in his room and didn't come out for a week. I called him every day for months."

The worship leader, now looking cheery enough, asked us to hold hands and pray. "We bind the powers of darkness," he said. "If there is anything in the body that is contrary to Jesus' plan, heal it. We plead for you to do mighty signs and wonders."

"Come, fire of God," he said, over and over, accompanied by cheers from the congregation. "Don't let us be lukewarm, but hot."

It was a far cry from Woodmen Valley. "That's the safe church," Haggard said.

"I was going to talk about prophecy," said Haggard when he got up to preach. "But after that front-page story this morning I decided not to be controversial."

He started with reconciliation—not just the personal reconciliation that comes readily to the lips of conservative Christians, but reconciliation between men and women, between whites and Native Americans, whites and blacks. He had had his own experience of that, he said, and that was why he wouldn't be at the main service that day. He would be washing the feet of Calvin Johnson, pastor of Solid Rock Christian Center, the black church with which New Life is linked.

"When Calvin told me he wanted to wash my feet," Haggard told his congregation, "I said, 'Oh, no, Calvin, you don't have to do that. Come on, let's go out and eat.' I didn't know what washing feet communicated in his culture. But then in Orlando I saw a footwashing, and it started to dawn on me that Calvin was trying to express his church's love and submission and honor and respect for our church. So I said to Calvin, 'I am coming to your church, to your biggest service, and I am going to wash your feet and the feet of your leadership in front of the congregation.

"It is important," Haggard said, "to be grateful and humble about what Jesus has done. Humility and gratitude are the greatest antidote against the wickedness of the human heart."

He ended his sermon with an altar call. "Some of you have gotten away from the Lord. But you don't have to live an aimless way of life. You can live a life that is the best God has planned for you.

Make your way into the aisles; come on home; come back to the Lord."

The people who dribbled forward—there weren't many—seemed deeply moved: a woman in a business suit with tears running down her cheeks, a teen-aged boy with a punk haircut and eyes red from crying. In front of me stood a huge barefooted old woman in a long orange dress who put her hands on the boy's head and prayed for him.

"It's livelier at the main service," Haggard said as we raced to his car. On the drive, he seemed determined to shake my liberal preconceptions. He resolutely refused to be shocked by the Jesus Seminar. "We can't ever know for sure what Jesus said, so you might as well vote on it as anything." And he confided, with the air of one making an astonishing revelation, "something I don't say often—I believe it is possible for people who do not come to Christ to be saved."

"Haggard doesn't match the culture he's in," one local had told me. And certainly the open-mindedness on display in the car fit oddly with Haggard's enjoyment of the service at Solid Rock where, as we came in, they were praying for the conversion of the Hindus.

But he had indeed shaken my prejudices. Even as my hackles rose at the idea that Hindus needed to be converted, I found myself moved by the prayer leader's compassion for the Hindus of Colorado Springs. Help them to feel welcome, he asked; ease their loneliness; protect them from prejudice and bitterness; and give us opportunities to serve them.

On the drive, Haggard had been musing about his relationship with Solid Rock's pastor. Johnson had grown up at St. John's Baptist, the biggest black church in town, where he was the star pupil and surrogate son of Vincent Proby, that church's pastor and a longtime Springs civil rights activist. But as an adult, Johnson had become a Pentecostal and a friend and follower of Haggard.

The tale was Colorado Springs church history writ small, Haggard had told me. "During the civil rights movement, St. John's was the place to be," he had said. "They were involved in everything, and everybody used to want to know what Pastor Proby thought. Then all us white guys from out of town waltz in and suddenly everybody is flocking to us. We're exploding with growth, and Pastor Proby is barely hanging on. He is feeling abandoned and bitter."

Haggard told Johnson's congregation about his refusal to have his feet washed. "I'm a white boy from Indiana, and I was raised Presbyterian," he said. "What do I know about washing feet?"

"But God is calling up a spirit of reconciliation," he went on. "And Pastor Proby is on my heart. After I have washed Calvin's feet, I want to go with him and any of you that want to come to St. John's and in that spirit of reconciliation wash Pastor Proby's feet."

Back in the car, Haggard seemed to be having second thoughts—or at least a fit of nerves. "It's a much more formal service than ours," he fretted, "and Pastor Proby doesn't take well to being interrupted."

Like a character in a nursery rhyme, Haggard had picked up followers at each stop, so by now we were four cars full. When the procession marched though a back door at St. John's and down the aisle, with a man carrying a basin and towels bringing up the rear, silence fell. Every head in the sanctuary turned our way.

Proby, an immensely tall, frail, elderly man, greeted Haggard and Johnson courteously, and listened to their request. "I accept," he said. "But before I allow you to wash my feet, I have a word to say. I need to ask your forgiveness too, for my anger and ungenerosity."

Perhaps they didn't know, he went on, that he had recently had a bypass operation, and then a stroke. "The devil was fighting for my soul, but God finally sent him away, saying 'Enough.'

"If God raises a man like that, it means something," he declared, his voice rising. "It means *enough* selfishness, and *enough* resentment, and *enough* division. I have treated you nice, Ted, but not like a brother, because I kept thinking God has allowed you to accomplish in thirteen years what I haven't been able to do in forty. But now we will work and worship together.

"And Calvin," he said to Johnson, who had fallen on the floor at his feet, "I let go of you. I endorse your ministry."

"A lot of people thanked me as we left," Haggard said later, "but I'm not sure they even know what they were thanking me for. It was just that there was a real power of God there, and all of us felt it."

I had left the church struggling with two equally strong and contradictory convictions: that many of Haggard's theological views are dead wrong, and that true, unexpected healing had taken place in that church.

Later, I told Haggard about my mixed reaction. "That's because it's not *about* right and wrong," he said. "It's about life and death."

When Haggard and I finally sat down for lunch, late that afternoon, it seemed to me that the long morning we had shared gave our conversation an unusual intensity.

He had commented, in his sermon, about the sins of parachurch groups and TV evangelists, constantly demanding money from church members and giving little in return. Is he opposed to them? He shares their general social outlook, he said, but his relationship with the organizations themselves is edgy. He told me he tried to keep the Christian Coalition out of Colorado Springs. "I don't believe you can politicize the gospel," he said. "The Nazis did, and the South Africans. It's always a mistake."

And he insisted he supports the Supreme Court's decision on school prayer, though he thinks it's wrong—and not what the court meant—to keep religion out of education. "Government is people, and people are religious. Rather than be exclusive, we ought to be inclusive," he stated with the certainty of one who believes that in a fair fight, his team would win. "I think it would be fantastic to have every religion come in and give its best pitch."

Haggard was one of the few people I met in Colorado Springs who talked about the Bible in terms of stories, instead of rules. At New Life, he told me, they urge new Christians to start with a child's Bible. "Yes, the Bible is instructional," he said. "But it's instructional not like a textbook, but like a storybook, through the examples and stories of other people's relationship and encounters with God. Sure, Paul developed a theology, and so did John, to an extent—but those guys who try to put the book of Revelation on a chart. . . ."

In the three sermons he'd preached that day, Haggard had made no attempt to explicate the Bible. But that didn't matter, he said. "I taught thousands of verses of scripture by portraying gratefulness and thankfulness. I didn't have to read every verse and have them memorize them to get there. I taught it by modeling it. That's the way Jesus would teach it."

He started talking about Adam and Eve. "The tree of the knowledge of good is just as deadly as the tree of the knowledge of evil. Lots of people pursue goodness in their churches and in their Bibles, and they're still dead."

I asked what seems to be, for every conservative Christian, the crucial question: "Are they saved?" But Haggard dismissed it.

"I don't know," he said. "That's not my issue. My issue is that they discover his life. I'm concerned about the impartation of life, and that's a very subtle spiritual dynamic. After all, the tree of knowledge is satisfying. Remember? When the serpent came to Eve, he said, 'Don't you want to be more like God?' We have a value system that makes that satisfying. The tree of knowledge makes you think you've found life in a religious system.

"'They think by calling me Lord, Lord, they're saved, but they don't know me,'" he went on, paraphrasing Jesus. "Jesus goes to great efforts to do away with systems like that. 'Here's the way you've got to do it,' Jesus says. 'You've got to eat me, and drink me.' You've got to ingest Jesus into you, and that's what happens when you pray the word. But it's always by faith and it's always a mystery. For any man to say to another that you've gained life . . ."

Haggard is not antisystem, he insisted; he has more rules for Bible teachers than Tomberlin does. They have to use a Pentecostal edition of the New International Version and they have to support the church's theology, whether they agree with it or not.

But knowing God is not a matter of information, but of experience, he says. "You saw that today in Calvin's heart. Calvin fell on the platform because the kingdom of God was invading his

heart. That's the kind of experience that every major Bible character had. Any dynamic relationship has emotion, passion, and
fear, including the one with God. Yes, the Bible is a book; yes, it
is ideas. And I'm all for mental exercise—but only when it leads
to a relationship of life."

As I explored New Life further, though, I began to wonder if
Haggard had painted a full picture. It was a look at the book he'd
given me that first made me queasy. *Primary Purpose*, it's called,
Making It Hard for People to Go to Hell from Your City. The first
chapter gives a detailed description of vicious demonic attacks
Haggard says his ministry has endured. True, there's a lot of sensible advice about viewing others charitably and not getting hung
up in doctrinal details, but still. . . .

And judging from the Bible studies I sat in on, if Haggard has
been modeling to his congregation the openness and passion for
story that he displayed to me, it hasn't sunk in with everyone.
Take my visit to a group studying the first chapter of Paul's letter to the Philippians.

The small house on the well-watered grounds of the Air Force
Academy is neat as a pin. Jim, the leader, apologizes for the small
size of his group tonight; several members are out of town, and
the only person here, besides Jim and his wife Ellen, is Ted,
barely out of his teens, wearing a Hawaiian shirt and the buzz
haircut of a serviceman. Even in its shrunken state, though, Jim
runs his group with a heavy hand.

"What is Paul most concerned about in verse 18?" he asks.
When the answers he gets—that Christ is preached, or that
Christ is exalted in his (Paul's) body—don't satisfy him, he provides the right one. "Yes, he's glad Christ is being talked about,"
he says, "but he is most concerned that Christ is glorified through
his example. For Christians, hopefully, it is our first and foremost
desire, no matter what we're doing, in our homes, or jobs, or relationships, that we would glorify Christ."

He moves on to the next verse. "What does he mean by 'to live
is Christ, and to die is gain'?"

"Would that mean that what Christ wants him to do is live,

though he would desire to die because he would be with the Lord?" asks Ellen. "See what I mean? If God wanted to take him now, he would be with Christ."

"You're jumping ahead," Jim scolds. "Sorry," she apologizes.

"'To die is gain' obviously means that he knows what reward is on the other side," Jim explains. "He may have heard people testify or have read how those who were clinically dead came back to life and told of meeting the Lord and walking in heaven."

In the Bible studies I've participated in, this conflation of present-day perspective with the first-century text is a cardinal sin. But there's something attractive about the way Jim assumes that Paul had access to the near-death books of the twentieth century. Like a medieval painter, he is plunking the Bible into his own century.

"How many Christians look at it that way?" asks Ellen with a troubled face. "Our children don't want to die. They want to grow up and get married and have children, even though we've told them what it is going to be like."

"It's human nature," says the young serviceman. "I imagine Paul as being above us."

"Be careful about thinking he's superhuman," Jim warns. "He still had a nature like ours, but of course God gave him an extra measure of faith and of insight so he could write these letters to us."

They get into a wrangle over whether it would be selfish of Paul to choose death. "Was the choice his?" asks Jim. Oh, no, that would be suicide, says Ellen.

"I think the Lord was giving him the choice," Jim insists.

But she stands up for herself, fetching another translation to see if there's ammunition there. "We'd have to read things into it, that he was sick or contemplated suicide. Why would Christ give him a choice? He hasn't ministered to kings yet." (She's referring to the risen Christ's prediction, in the book of Acts, that Paul would bring Christ's name before Gentiles and kings.)

"We already spoke about that," Jim reminds her. "He spoke to the governor of Jerusalem and Judea."

She gives in. "What do you think?"

"He knows God appointed him as apostle to the Gentiles, and Peter and John were for the Jews. They weren't going to be able to come in and follow up with his churches, so he said, 'Lord, I need to stay around a little longer for your sake.'"

He moves on. "From this text, and others, what happens when you die?"

"Well, in the movies, you see this long line at the pearly gates," says Ted. "But I don't think you sit in line. I don't think you have time to plan. As soon as you go, you're at his feet."

From Paul's writings, Jim says, "it's clear that the spirit joins the Lord once the body dies. There are many passages in Jesus' teaching, Paul's writing, and the book of Revelation that talk about a new body. Later on, in chapter 3, he talks about that new body. Any questions on that?"

I am tempted to challenge him; "new body" is a Pauline concept never used by Jesus. But this wasn't the only time I was to hear Paul's words put into Jesus' mouth, or vice versa. If you believe God wrote it all, you don't waste time distinguishing Jesus' theology from Paul's.

"Do we have bodies like our mortal bodies when we go to heaven?"

I am fascinated by their fascination with this issue. The early Christians expected the world to end at any instant, so for them it was a pressing concern. Most liberal Christians, though, regard the so-called Last Things—death, judgment, hell, and heaven—as an embarrassing relic of a primitive faith.

"We know demons don't have bodies like ours; they're spiritual beings," Jim says. "So are angels. But angels can materialize to appear before us. When they do, is that a body? Something we can touch? In heaven I don't think we will need a body. But when the Lord comes back to earth to reign, and we reign with him, he will give us new, incorruptible bodies. We won't be affected by the elements. We'll be able to fly."

"I'm getting all goose-bumpy thinking about it," says Ted.

Jim starts talking about why he left the Roman Catholic Church. "They never taught me that I could know I was going to heaven," he says. "By believing in the Lord Jesus Christ and fol-

lowing him, we can know. What a gamble to risk eternity on hoping for the best.

"How does God enable you to suffer for his sake?" he asks.

"Well," says Ted, "like by showing you good times when you're
going through bad times. You can see the light at the end of the
tunnel."

"Have you suffered?" asks Ellen solicitously.

"Me? No, I've never been in that situation."

"Neither have I," she responds. "I wouldn't consider people
making fun of me suffering."

"It is supernatural," Jim says. "Like POWs getting through
years of torture. How do they do it? With the Lord's help. They
think about something great waiting on the other side, and about
people praying for them. Like my friend Dave who's been trying
to get his daughter back from his ex-wife who's not a Christian.
It's been a tremendous trial, but God is faithful."

If there was too little particularity for me in the Woodmen Valley Bible studies, there is too much here. They are indeed devour-
ing the book; but is this what Haggard meant by ingesting it?

Many years ago, at the urging of a friend who hoped, I think,
to rescue me from what she considered my constricting Christianity, I read a couple of books on the teachings of the Russian
mystic Gurdjieff. It was a sunny Saturday afternoon, and when I
emerged from my bedroom after a few hours in Gurdjieff's company I felt I'd escaped from an opium den into a clean and light-
filled world. Nothing in that chintz-covered living room
resembled an opium den, but I had the same sense of having, for
a few hours, lived in an alien world so powerful it almost blocked
out my own. To me, the Bible is a voice from a time and culture
whose viewpoint and assumptions are almost as different from
my own as those of God must be. My recognition of that distance
is part of what allows the Bible to come alive for me.

For this group, though, there was no distance—or at least
none that they were aware of. Paul was writing his letters not to
distant, wrangling congregations, but to them, and Jesus' coming
again was as urgent a concern for them as it was for first-century
Christians. Where I have to struggle for sympathy, they, without

struggling, found an easy immediacy. It was hard not to feel that they knew something I didn't. Whether I wanted that knowledge was another question.

A few days later I drove over to a corporate campus on the south end of town to visit a lunchtime Bible study organized by Nate Peachey, a New Life member who works for a computer-chip maker. Not everyone in this group goes to New Life, he told me as we headed to the cafeteria to pick up lunch—foot-long, four-inch-high heroes. We sit around a conference table, strug-gling to get our mouths around our sandwiches. There's only one woman in the group.

I am as odd a specimen here as the people I'd met the other night were to me. Do Episcopalians believe in water baptism? they ask. Infant baptism? What is the Eucharist?

And—most important question of all—How do Episcopalians know when they are saved?

I hear in that anxious query two questions: Do Episcopalians have the direct encounter with God that for the questioner offered the only religious certainty? And do Episcopalians say those words of surrender, caricatured as "accepting Jesus as your personal savior," that for him were the only guarantee of heaven?

When the true answer lies somewhere between "sometimes" and "sort of," it's hard to put it into words that will speak to some-one for whom the true answer is always "yes" or "no."

"When we are saved isn't a big issue for us," I say, feeling inept. "We focus more on baptism making us part of the body of Christ."

He looks bewildered.

The topic is Luke's parable of the good Samaritan, and Peachey starts with a historical overview of the relationship between Israel and Judah and the low opinion both nations had of Samaritans. "If they were going from Galilee to Jerusalem," he says, "they would go across the Jordan to avoid Samaria." For Jesus to take the route through Samaria was very odd, he points out. "Why do you think he used a Samaritan in the story?"

The question provokes the first of many outbursts from the

man who had wondered what the Eucharist is. He may not know my theology, but he sure knows his. He barely stops to breathe.

"In Leviticus it talks about love thy neighbor as thyself. What Christ is doing is taking the Old Testament, which is Christ concealed, and transferring it into the New Testament, which is Christ revealed. It's the same thing when they bring the adulterous woman; he's explaining the meaning of the Old Covenant law, which is that it's not only adultery when committed in the flesh but when committed in the mind. He's putting the lawyer on the spot, but the whole purpose of the Old Testament law is to show that we couldn't keep the law in our present state and needed the Christ, the Christ that God speaks about in Micah. Love of God and love of neighbor, setting aside the Old Covenant and bringing forth the New Covenant, all these things are encompassed in that. Somebody asked me what's particular about the Sabbath, and what I found out was Christ came as high priest under the old law, but when he was crucified, the New Testament came into being and at no time after that do you see any mention of people honoring the Sabbath or keeping the Sabbath; the Sabbath is a rest and we enter into God's rest, when you love the Lord your God with all your heart, you dwell in the shelter of the Most High; everything else—murder, adultery, fornication, rage—all those things lead to death. . . ."

It's a wild amalgam of Luke, Romans, Hebrews, Micah, Psalms, and half-a-dozen other biblical books I can't place, all forced through a dispensationalist sieve. I'd found a lot of this in my Internet explorations, but this is the first time I have ever come upon it in person, and I wonder how on earth they are going to get him to stop.

"After Matthew, Mark, Luke, and John the Sabbath really isn't mentioned anymore?" asks one man, turning to Peachey, who quickly pulls them back to the Good Samaritan. "If you'll notice at the end of the story, the expert in the law doesn't use the word *Samaritan.* He says, 'the one who had mercy on him.' It's interesting."

"That's always been my favorite parable, and my dad's too," says an older man. "One of the reasons my late father thought so poorly of Christians was that he experienced this parable. His part of West Virginia was very, very hilly, and one day he drove the car partway off a cliff. A couple of prominent church members drove right by, and then another rough-hewn character who hadn't been to church in sixty years towed him off the cliff. I think that's where a lot of Christians today fall short. No matter what they think or believe, what they do is the only thing anybody sees."

"There's a bit of tension in the story," says Peachey, "and it challenges us to rethink the way we interact with people. There's two things I'd like to bring up—I fail to understand how churchmen in the South during the slave period could not only live with slavery, but could even prove, so to speak, that it was OK. And second, how could we have things like what are known as the various great awakenings in our early history and still treat the Indians with the cruelty we have treated them with?"

"Their spirits had been born again but their minds and conscience and thoughts and feelings hadn't," says the dispensationalist, and he is off again (more briefly this time) with complex distinctions between being a new man in Christ and living in Christ. "I don't know the condition of the hearts and souls of the people making treaties with the Indians, but some people come with a gospel that looks like Christ but the truth isn't in them."

"They focused on the Old Testament, not the New," says another.

"In what ways do we do some of those very same things and not realize it?" asks Peachey.

The man whose father didn't think much of Christians chimes in. "I can offer an answer, but not one you want to hear. I believe as a historian that, until the kingdom of God comes, there are some brutish truths. No family, no clan, no nation can have anything except what it is strong and powerful enough to take from another, and no family or clan or nation can keep what they have unless they're powerful enough to keep it from another. Had the Canadians been powerful enough, we would be speaking French."

In one way, anyhow, the conservative Christians of Colorado Springs do not resemble their first-century counterparts: they are anything but pacifist. But few of them face the contradiction as bluntly as this, and he's making them squirm.

"It may be truth," says one, "but it's no excuse for personal behavior."

"You can read the Bible, you can believe in the Bible, but basically human nature is still dark," responds his opponent. "Europeans had been murdering Europeans for thousands of years, so why would they be deterred when they met a group of people even more different from them?"

"But mercy has to triumph over judgment," said the man who wondered how Episcopalians know they are saved. "It's like me thinking about Episcopalians, 'Are they thinking about salvation in the right way?' It's not my business to judge. Daily you have to have mercy and grace, back and forth, for relationships to work."

Peachey tells a story Haggard had already told me. "Most of you know I grew up with Native American people, and there is a small sense in which they are my people. The Sand Creek massacre, which happened around here, is one of the darkest blotches on Colorado history. And at New Life, we went through a time of repentance and asking forgiveness for what happened back then. To me, at least, it's significant that a notable Christian church in the area would repent of what its ancestors did. There are things on a personal level that we're involved in, past or present, where we don't realize until it's all over our need for repentance."

He has touched a chord. "There's a real need for reconciliation with the Native Americans," says one man. "Where I grew up you didn't pick up a stranded Indian along the road. You figured he was drunk, and wanted nothing to do with it."

The one woman speaks up for the first time. "I have a great-grandmother who was a full-blooded Cherokee. Her own family didn't want to go out with her because of her red skin. What would Jesus have said to people in our situation?"

"It's like Ted preached about kindness," says the man who had puzzled over my salvation. "You draw more flies with honey than arsenic. Kindness has a wonderful place in the Christian life."

For my next New Life Bible study, I go back up Academy Road, this time to one of the new housing developments growing like weeds in that part of town—so fast the developers haven't had time to think of enough names. Left on Somerset, then right on Somerhill. A handful of people, another chintz-covered room, flickering candles, and soft lighting. When John, the leader, opens the session with the reading of several psalms, it feels more like a service than a class.

They are beginning the letter to the Ephesians, and tonight's session is an overview. "Our salvation is part of God's eternal plan, and you see that woven through the first three chapters," says John. "How is the mystery here different from Colossians?"

"In Colossians," responds his wife, "it was Christ in you, the hope of glory."

"And what is it here?"

"That Jews and Gentiles would be equal, which hadn't been revealed to that point."

"That purpose can be illustrated all the way back to the garden of Eden," John says, though his explanation that God established a worship center in Eden doesn't seem to prove the point.

"Why do you think all the main cities that were the start of the church are no longer Christian places?" asks another member. The question, though I don't realize it yet, is a setup, but John postpones answering it and goes back to explaining his system.

"What it comes down to," he says, "is that the manifold wisdom of God should now be known to the levels of angelic authority that are out there. This is top-secret doctrine. God didn't let the angels know what was going on."

Their laps are filled with notebooks and Bibles, but the pace is languid.

"Here's how I've heard this described," says John, asking his wife to stand for a visual illustration. "God loved to have fellowship with man," he says, hugging her. "When we go to heaven our crowns will be made of his manifest presence.

"But when man fell, look what happened," he goes on, pushing his wife away. "The holy God couldn't even stand in the presence of man, so what would happen if the holy God tried to hug and have fellowship with him? It would consume him. But God desired to reach out, and his eternal purpose in Christ Jesus was to crown the church with glory." They both sit down again.

"There is a living-in-personal-holiness piece of this," John says. "Instead of nurturing the old man, you are being filled with the Spirit. And when you are filled with the Spirit, there is no place to be domineering over another person. Then it goes right on to the next thing of wives being subject to their husbands. But it doesn't say wives be a doormat, or a punching bag. And what does it say for the man to do? Submit to Christ and love and nurture your wife, being under submission to her because she has a place in the marriage."

They move on to the writer's injunction to put on the full armor of God. John has really got this worked out. "It's no coincidence," he says, "that this comes last, after personal holiness and relations with your wife and children and employer. When all that is right, then you can stand in the place of the evil one."

"The first part is a training manual, and the last part is marching orders," chimes in another member.

"Exactly right," John says.

Then he takes up the question he'd dismissed earlier: why the first places to hear the gospel are no longer Christian. "If you look at where Buddha came down, they are still Buddhist there, and Mecca is still Muslim. But Christianity disappeared in the fifth century out of what is now Israel, and in the eleventh or twelfth century it started to disappear out of Asia Minor. I have my own opinion on that, but let's look at the letter."

Since all Paul's letters were passed around from church to church, why were they addressed to a single church at all? he asks. Why not just to everybody? "Did the Spirit have a purpose?"

He jumps to the description, in Acts, of Paul's visit to Ephesus, when he almost got run out of town because his preaching threatened the livelihood of the artisans who supplied the great temple of Artemis (known to the Romans as Diana). But John emphasizes not Paul's narrow escape, but the baptism of the Spirit he brought to Christians there who had until then been baptized only with water. "This was the third Pentecost that appeared here," he says. "All of Turkey had been saturated with the gospel, and there were what we call power encounters occurring along with this proclamation of the gospel. It looks like there's just an explosion of the word coming out of Ephesus. Look at it today, and the city is in ruins. There's not a Christian probably within a hundred miles."

And why? His answer sticks pieces of Acts, Ephesians, and Revelation together with gobs of imaginative glue.

"The image of Diana at Ephesus *fell down* out of heaven," he says. "Have you heard the term Queen of Heaven? It's Artemis. That was the spirit reigning over Ephesus. And Paul swept it away. But look at Revelation. The *first* letter to the churches is to Ephesus, and it says, 'Don't lose your first love.' That's what I believe happened. There was an evil principality that was still there, though it had been weakened, dispelled, by the prevailing word of God. But the church of Ephesus lost its first love, and its lamp stand was removed. The evil spirit, finding it swept, came back in and dominated. I believe that Islam is a curse on Christianity. Did you know that Mohammed's mother was a devout Eastern Orthodox Christian? But he entered into a church with his mother, and he saw the idolatry that had so filled the Eastern Orthodox church that he sought his own revelation. The church in Ephesus had gone and committed idolatry. It had lost its first love."

He is in tears now, choking up and beating his chest. "I don't understand God's plan," he says with a deep sigh, "how the kingdom of God could so permeate a place, and yet the enemy gets a foothold and pushes Christianity out. But God's eternal purpose says I'm going to zing right in here where this spirit rules and reigns. Paul did it once, but the church in this day is going to do it again. And next year, in Operation Queen's Palace, the church is going to reclaim Ephesus." He is almost beyond speech, and his wife is in tears as well. "That is the eternal purpose of the church," he says, "and not just for Ephesus. The *eternal purpose* . . ."

The only science fiction novels that have ever grabbed me are those of C. S. Lewis. In one of them, *Perelandra,* the narrator meets an angel and finds it a shattering experience. "Here at last was a bit of that world . . . which I had always supposed that I loved and desired, breaking through and appearing to my senses: and I didn't like it, I wanted it to go away."

Well, here was the stuff of those novels, the cosmic struggle of the powers and principalities, jumping off the page at me, and I felt very much the same.

What made it more discomfiting was that I couldn't even brush it off as unbiblical. Paul's letters, the letter to the Ephesians (which is probably not by Paul), and above all the book of Revelation understand battle with supernatural powers as simply a given of doing God's business in the universe.

For that matter, so does Haggard. When I went on-line to find out if there really *was* an Operation Queen's Palace, I discovered that not only is it real, but its leader is Peter Wagner, Haggard's colleague in the Prayer Center and the author of an introduction to his book—the book which, I now recalled, gave detailed instructions for fending off demonic attacks.

Liberals I met in Colorado Springs looked nervous when I talked about the conservatives I was meeting; they feared my fascination might push me over the border into enemy territory. But what I was experiencing had nothing to do with conversion, or at least not with the conversion they feared. It was the tossed-in-a-blanket feeling of having my categories scrambled beyond recognition.

Chapter 9

Springs Community Church,
Colorado Springs, CO

Precept Ministries,
Chattanooga, TN

O ne of the things that puzzled me about the conservative Christians I was meeting was that they seemed to have no experts. When I had written an article about the Bible for *Mother Jones* magazine, I had had no trouble finding liberal experts. They know each other; they quote each others' books; they appear on the same television programs and trek around the country making the same speaking tour stops. The church that had Marcus Borg at its big weekend event one year will most likely invite John Dominic Crossan or John Spong the next.

But there didn't seem to be a conservative Bible-teaching circuit. The big names in the conservative world, the ones that can be depended on to draw a crowd, are preachers, evangelists, and politicians; they aren't Bible teachers.

Or so I'd thought. But at Springs Community Church I discovered I had been looking in the wrong places. If you want to find a conservative biblical celebrity, you don't go to conferences and speeches; you head for the videotape section of the nearest Christian bookstore.

Perched among unfinished building sites on the very edge of the plateau, Springs Community Church almost falls off the map of Colorado Springs. There's nothing beyond it but the road sweeping down to the Great Plains. The smallest church I visited and the first one that belonged to a denomination (the Reformed Church in America, the denomination of Robert Shuller and Norman Vincent Peale), it takes a far greater interest in social problems than either Woodmen Valley or New Life. For anything connected with poverty, I'd been told, evangelical pastors turned to Springs Pastor Steve Brooks for advice. The day I attended services, Brooks was living up to his advance notices; he was trying to raise money, and volunteers, for a ministry to single mothers.

Many Springs Community members are intimidated by the Bible, Brooks told me when we talked, and the church has struggled, not always successfully, to change that. "We've done poorly in the traditional adult, Sunday morning hour-long class. There's enough people who fancy that would be a great idea, and we start with thirty people, but eight weeks later, there are only six or seven. My analysis is that it doesn't offer enough of an experience."

One offering that had been successful was a women's Bible study that used books and tapes by somebody named Kay Arthur. "They study on their own, then they meet in small groups, and then they watch a videotape of her speaking. She teaches principles backed up from scripture." Currently they were doing a study on healing life's hurts, he told me, and I was just in time for the last class.

"The whole point of this study," Alice, the leader, told the twenty-odd women in the classroom, "is that through it all, God has been weaving his truth around you and your circumstances. Now you come to that place where you say, what are you going to do then? We have really gotten targeted with forgiveness. I don't know about you, but man, I like to never got through this lesson."

"I didn't," one woman confesses to her neighbor, sotto voce.

"We had tons of scripture," Alice says. "I was going, 'enough, already.'" She seems determined to show herself no smarter than the students, and I wonder if she feels that way, or if it's a technique, meant to reassure those who have bogged down along the way.

"As we looked at the scripture, one of the first things we looked at was the fact God gets angry. Why?"

The answers tumble out: sin, injustice, disappointment, betrayal, disobedience, speaking against your neighbor. . . .

"Is it OK for you to get angry at God?"

"When my little girl died," says one woman, "I told God every day how angry I was, because he could have given her the breath of life if he'd chosen to. I never sensed, in my relation with him, that it was not OK. It was an unfair thing and a sad thing and it was OK to be angry at it."

"What about anger against someone else?" Alice asks.

"If it's justified—"

"Justifiable anger? It sounds like justifiable homicide."

The woman who had lost her child jumps in again. "I read in the paper about a young mom who six months ago was accused of crushing the skull of her baby girl, and on Mother's Day she stabbed the baby to death. I'm angry about that. I think those are the kinds of things God expects us to be angry about. Starving people in the Sudan or Zaire—we're supposed to be angry that evil is in the world."

"Do you really think God planned on that baby dying?" asks a woman with long red hair and an eager face. "It's hard to understand why he would . . . of course he had no control over how the baby died . . . but was he only destined to live that short time, and for his mother to take that on herself?"

"But we saw the molested child in Kay's book. God is all-seeing and he saw it. It's OK to say, 'This is hard for me, Lord.' But if we obey scripture, we believe he has a plan we can't see."

The subject outstrips their vocabulary; as categories, "OK" and "not OK" are hardly adequate for the age-old dilemma of theodicy.

"Let's look at Psalm 27," says Alice. "We get a lot of answers in this one. This guy was really struggling, and he went to the Lord with his anger and said, 'I don't get it.' God showed him the end of the evil, and then he said, 'OK, I understand, I can move on.' What does the Lord give you to help you with anger?"

They've done the lesson and the answers come quickly: wait; rest; trust; wait patiently; do good.

"Look at James 1, specifically 19–26," says Alice. "What does he tell you in this passage?"

"The first admonition, to be quick to listen, changes the focus from your reaction to what the other person is saying," notes a woman who hasn't spoken much.

"I wish I knew then what I know now," says one of the older women in the group. "Back when I had kids I was so afraid of losing the war that I never let them win even a skirmish. And most of the time I couldn't remember later what had triggered it."

"We're not sweating it when our son walks around with long hair," responds another. "He's seen the picture of his dad in the band."

"Is he body-piercing yet?"

They are asking the questions of Job and getting the answers of James—it's not a fair exchange.

After a refreshment break, we settle down to watch Arthur's tape. She looks to be in her well-kept fifties, with the down-to-earth, self-deprecating charm of the southerner she is. She illustrates the way emotions work—a subject on which she is as canny as any psychiatrist—with homely stories about stage fright and fights with her husband. "We are psychosomatic beings," she says. "If you carry your anger over to the next day, it will affect your body."

But she treats the Bible as if it were a blackboard, not a book about human beings. Outbursts of uncontrolled anger are sinful, she says. But the Bible is full of them, from Cain who killed his brother ("stuffed anger," Arthur says, "like the guy who opened fire in McDonald's") to the apostle Paul, whose outbursts—including wishing his opponents would castrate themselves—she does not mention. She flips through the books of the Bible, from Genesis to Isaiah to Hebrews and back again, as though all the writers were in absolute agreement.

"You have to look beyond the situation that causes the anger to the God that is in control of the situation," she says.

Remember that the situation that caused the anger has no eternal existence. "It's hard to get dead men to respond," she jokes, "and your natural self is dead."

You can afford to have compassion on those who anger you, she goes on. "That person is going to spend eternity in hell, unless they're saved—and you're not."

For all her psychological gloss, Arthur comes off like Job's comforters. "Slay your anger as a sacrifice to God," she says. "Say, 'Lord, if it pleases you, it pleases me.'"

After the class, I talked with two of its members, Lynn Vander Horck and Mary Beth Hollinger. Both of them grew up believing good deeds got you to heaven, a view both have since rejected.

"We did go to church," said Vander Horck. "But I thought it was hypocritical. My father molested me and my sister—and he taught Sunday school." She became a born-again Christian at sixteen. "I didn't walk a true walk with the Lord at that time, but I knew my salvation was intact."

Hollinger's family were atheists; what faith she had as a child she learned from her grandmother. She was converted at twenty, but it was shaky. "I started reading the Bible in the Old Testament," she said, "and when I saw God's judgment on their sin, I figured, 'Oops, I've sinned; I'm going to be separate from God,' and I got discouraged and kept on sinning."

Half-a-dozen years later, though, she was looking at a Bible on her sister's coffee table, and a light bulb went on. "This was God's word, what he wanted to have in the book. Not everything in there might be a statement of truth, but it was all true statements."

"The Bible is the divine word of God," said Vander Horck. "It is not just a bunch of stories. What is written in it is directly from God."

Both women believe the Bible will lead them to God's will for them. "I write questions down and try to think on them," Hollinger said. "I wait and sometimes I feel like the Lord has given me understanding, and sometimes I don't. Or I will ask the Lord to give me direction, and citations will come into my head."

That's risky, Vander Horck said. "If you're not obedient, you can just pick a scripture that sounds good."

"I think it's the motivation," her friend responded. "If you're truly seeking truth and an answer from God, that's one thing, but we can want to justify something we've already decided, and find something that suits our purpose."

"If more people were involved in studying and learning from the Bible, we would have fewer problems," Vander Horck added. Tolerance is a good thing, she said, but it's gone too far. "We all have different frames of reference and different backgrounds. I know I can read a chapter I read five years ago and have a totally different reaction. I'm not trying to shove my politics down somebody's throat. I'm just saying that absolutes exist in the word of God in terms of how we should behave."

When I asked whether the Bible has made a difference in their lives, Vander Horck spoke quickly, her voice shaking with held-back tears. "I was really a mess, and didn't know it," she said. "I was very dysfunctional, controlling, codependent. I didn't realize the path I had taken."

And now? "I feel well. I'm emotionally stable; I'm mentally healthy; I'm spiritually secure. I'd say"—her eyes brightened in astonishment as she claimed the word—"I'd say I'm happy. I couldn't say that even a year ago."

Hollinger chimed in. "For me, the biggest thing is knowing I am loved and accepted—and now *I'm* going to cry. I can remember feeling purposeless and empty, and it's been a big change for me knowing that the God that created the universe loves me and has a purpose for my life."

Curious about the approach to the Bible that had made such a difference to these women, I went looking for Kay Arthur material in the Family Bookshop, one of the biggest Christian bookstores in town. From the front door, there was hardly a book in sight. The place was jammed with *stuff*—mugs with Bible verses, sentimental religious pictures, stained glass, wreaths with angels on them, cards for every imaginable occasion. And, of course, a wide selection of beaded bracelets carrying the letters WWJD:

What Would Jesus Do? The question stems from an 1896 religious classic, *In His Steps,* by Charles M. Sheldon. It's the story of a group of people who commit themselves, for one year, to doing only what they believe Jesus, in their situation, would do.

Given the plot, one would expect *In His Steps* to teem with Gospel verses and stories. But the Bible is hardly even mentioned. For all the talk about what Jesus would do, not one character in the book ever opens a Bible to see what he *did* do. As they decide (as most of them do) to work in missions, or to help the poor find employment—or, as a newspaper owner does, to stop publishing the paper on Sunday—their real dependence is not on the demanding, passionate healer and Sabbath-breaker who stalks the Gospels, but on the Holy Spirit, who speaks to their hearts in their own language.

Setting aside its Victorian, middle-class gloss, the world pictured in *In His Steps* holds a powerful appeal. Employers look out for the welfare of their workers; the rich contribute their goods and labor to serve the poor; and everyone is filled with the exhilaration of God's Spirit, united even in tribulation. It's a dream world very like the idealistic picture of the early church in Acts of the Apostles.

But it's half a world, not a whole one—a world in which God is a savior, but not a creator. The only acceptable motive for action in *In His Steps* is to bring others to Christ. The one artist in the group, a singer, turns down a concert tour in order to sing at revival meetings in the city's slums. Her would-be suitor, a writer, declines to join the group and becomes a hack, writing frivolous society novels.

In concert with *In His Steps,* I read *Experiencing God,* by Henry Blackaby. Blackaby is special assistant for prayer and spiritual awakening to the president of the Southern Baptist Convention's North American Mission Board. His book, I'd been told, is deeply influential in evangelical circles. Judging from its prominent placement here, it's at least popular. And the two books go together well; *Experiencing God* reads like an instruction manual for *In His Steps.*

The book's purpose is teach its readers how to develop a relationship with God. Spirituality may be the topic du jour in mainstream churches, but it has only recently come to the front burner among conservative Christians, who have more often emphasized correct belief than passionate feeling. But religion without feeling is a dry matter, and conservatives have flocked to books like Blackaby's that promise that they, like Moses, can meet God and know God's love for them.

At first glance, it's hard to see why. The cover of the book features an illustration of God as a fierce-looking old man whose ruddy face seems to be lit by the fires of hell. Not somebody I'd go to looking for love.

But once past the cover, Blackaby's book is sensible in almost every important way. He gives instructions for discerning whether an experience is of God that resemble, though in less detail, those of St. Ignatius. He warns against the self-deluding "name it and claim it" theology, popular in some conservative circles, which holds that every promise in scripture applies to everyone at all times; when you find something you want described in the Bible, just name it and claim it, and it's yours.

But the world in which this good advice is offered is as narrow as Sheldon's. The book is stuffed with anecdotes, but they all tell the same story: when God calls, he calls to mission work. After a while, I began to wonder just why Blackaby believed it was so important to wait to hear what God said before acting, since God always seemed to say the same thing. According to Blackaby, God's instructions differ only in the details: move to this state, not that; accept this job, not that one. (The notion, once suggested to me by a Jesuit friend, that "there are times when God says do what you like," is utterly foreign to Blackaby, for whom God points the way in the tiniest details of life, and expects instant obedience.)

Blackaby's book, in several different editions, stood out prominently in the book section, which I finally found at the back of the store. Kay Arthur was there too, with dozens of volumes. There were apocalyptic novels, though fewer than I expected, and long rows of romance novels and mysteries with a Christian slant. In cleansing their universe from the sins of the world, conservative Christians don't want to *miss* anything. They want escape literature just as much as the rest of us. Christian escape literature.

Even most of the Bibles on display were different from the ones I was used to seeing. Sure, the store carried most of the standard translations. More prominently displayed, though, were what I began to think of as the guided-tour Bibles. You could buy Kay Arthur's *Inductive Study Bible,* or Blackaby's *Experiencing God Bible,* or the *Full Life Bible,* the Pentecostal study Bible that New Life uses, or any of two dozen other Bibles that, one way or another, teach you what you are reading.

The guided Bible is not, of course, unique to the evangelical world or even to the Protestant one. Authorities of every age have feared what would happen if readers were allowed to approach the book without such explanations. But as liberals have adopted the techniques of science in their approach to the Bible, their Bibles have replaced highly opinionated commentary with an attempt at objectivity. In more conservative circles, the scientific approach is desecration. Beginning with the *Scofield Reference Bible,* first produced in 1909 by one Dr. C. I. Scofield to guide readers through what he insisted were only apparent inconsistencies to the one true, consistent, dispensationalist interpretation, they've felt an urgent need to shepherd readers along the path. And judging by the sales of these Bibles, readers feel an equally urgent need to be shepherded.

The *Scofield Bible* is still in print, and available in my local Barnes & Noble, so in the home of conservatism I expected it to be prominently displayed. But I could hardly find it. It was during my search that I realized what was truly curious about this store. It wasn't that the books were unfamiliar—the books in any seminary bookstore would be equally strange to me. It was that there was no history here.

I could find no books about the church's beginnings, or about the Reformation. I couldn't even find any specifically evangelical history: nothing about the great awakening that swept the country during the last century, or the Azuza revival in California that began the Pentecostal movement. Apart from the Bibles, the only book I found in the whole place that was less than about a dozen years old was *In His Steps*.

What the store did have, in abundance, was modern technology. An enormous children's section offered every imaginable form of religious video, game, and toy, including biblical action figures. The adult video section held shelves and shelves of tapes by Kay Arthur, T. D. Jakes, Chuck Swindoll, and many others, as well as videos of just about every book of the Bible and what seemed like every movie ever made (except for *The Last Temptation of Christ*) of the life of Jesus.

And the computer section! The only place you'd find a richer choice of digital Bible programs would be a seminary bookstore. If there. Only its price (six hundred dollars) saved me from succumbing to the temptation to walk out of there carrying, on a few computer disks, the original Greek and Hebrew texts of the Old and New Testament, dozens of English translations, and a library-full of concordances, commentaries, atlases, and theological documents.

The juxtaposition was still more evidence, if I needed more, of the immediacy with which the people I was meeting treat the Bible. Nobody would know, looking at the material for sale here, that the Bible is an ancient book whose long history of readers has held to diverse and often divergent interpretations. But it would be clear to them that it is a book so important that every tool of modern technology needs to be brought to the task of understanding its message. Reading the books for sale here, they would never hear that the Bible's message can be painfully unclear. But they would hear over and over again that understanding it is a matter of life and death.

In addition to the Blackaby and Sheldon books (and a mug illustrated with Colorado wildflowers under the admonition "Rejoice in the Lord always"), I left the bookstore with a copy of what seemed to be the introductory Kay Arthur book, *How to Study Your Bible*. One look told me why Alice had been so self-deprecating, so careful not to make anyone feel inferior, in introducing the week's lesson. Studying the Bible Kay Arthur's way is a lot of work.

Arthur follows the theory of a Shakespeare professor I had in college; to understand the work, he insisted, you first have to know it inside and out. His end-of-the-year objective exam was the work of an imaginative fiend.

Arthur calls her technique inductive Bible study. Armed with colored pens (sold in conjunction with her study Bible), the reader marks the speaker, the place, the audience, the most frequently used words, the subject of each section, and a myriad of other details, and then outlines first the book, then the sections within the book, and finally each paragraph.

The method is much more suitable for tracing a line of argument than it is for following a story or a vision, and indeed for Arthur, that's the point. "The Bible was written," she writes at the beginning of the book, "so that anyone who wants to know who God is and how they are to live in a way that pleases him can read it and find out."

Objectivity is a word Arthur uses often, and while it's easy to argue with her appropriation of the term, given the theological presuppositions that underlie everything she does, she has a point. Don't depend on others to interpret the Bible for you, she says over and over, and don't rely on what you want it to mean. See for yourself what it says. She teaches her readers to use concordances and Greek dictionaries, and even includes several appendixes on Greek verb forms and their subtleties. Set aside what you've been taught, she says, and figure it out yourself. You can do it, so claim your independence. To readers who fear that only an expert can make sense of the Bible, her books must come as a tonic.

Arthur is aware that she's demanding an enormous amount of work. Almost every chapter ends with a little pep talk addressed directly to the reader, whom she generally calls "friend" or "beloved."

"Are you concerned, my friend, that you are not going to come up with the right answers? Relax; don't panic . . . I always tell my students, 'Hangeth thou, in there!'"

Addressing readers who have had little or no literary education, she warns them against jumping to false conclusions because they don't recognize a metaphor when they see one. She devotes one entire chapter to figures of speech, and another to distinguishing among parables, allegories, types, and symbols. She points out that biblical authors write in different styles, from differing perspectives, and urges readers to take those factors into account when interpreting their words.

But her "objectivity" comes with fundamentalist strings. Scripture can be taken literally, she says, in its "natural, normal sense"—there are no hidden meanings. She enthusiastically points out instances where one biblical writer repeats another, but only to prove that God inspired both of them; in biblical writers as artists in their own right, she takes no interest at all. Scripture never contradicts itself, she insists. If it seems to, it's just because you've misunderstood something.

She instructs her students in irony. But she herself uses one of the most ironic remarks in the Bible, utterly seriously, as her slogan and title. "Precept upon Precept," she describes her method, and she calls her organization Precept Ministries. The phrase comes from the prophet Isaiah, who throws it in fury at his opponents. Since they won't listen to God, he says, God's word will be to them precept upon precept, line upon line, here a little, there a little—"that they may fall backward and be broken and snared."

And though Arthur insists that readers figure out the meaning for themselves, that meaning, in her universe, is single and absolute. Words like "accurate" and "correct" crop up frequently. In her chapter on figures of speech, for instance, she discusses Luke's account of the last supper, in which Jesus says, "This is my body which is given for you."

"Some believe," she writes, "that the bread actually becomes His body (the doctrine of transubstantiation); others believe that Jesus was simply using a *metaphor* and that the bread, therefore, is representative of His body. These differences occur because not all students of the Word adhere to the guidelines for interpreting figurative language." In other words, they don't know a metaphor when they see one.

Judging by Arthur's book, there is no room in her thinking for ambiguity or argument. But as I found out when I visited her headquarters in Chattanooga, Tennessee, to watch her teach, it's not quite that simple.

I happened to arrive on the day she was taping a lecture on chapters 12–14 of the first letter to the Corinthians, which includes Paul's glorious hymn to charity—and his notorious strictures on allowing women to speak in church. Arthur is a woman, as is the bulk of her audience. Even to these biblical literalists, Paul's words were not pleasant hearing.

If it weren't for the spreading parking lots, anybody driving the narrow, winding country roads north of Chattanooga and stumbling on the headquarters of Precept Ministries would think they'd come upon a cozy country bed and breakfast. Broad porches encircle the houses, which are furnished in Early Yield House—pine-paneled walls, pine furniture, rag rugs, ruffles, and chintz.

To give the tapes as much verisimilitude as possible, Arthur makes them in the same circumstances that viewers will see them; the audience does the homework and attends classes before trooping into the television studio to watch Arthur's lecture.

There are about thirty women in the classroom, all armed with notebooks and huge Bibles. Beverly Miller, a member of Arthur's staff, opens with a prayer, thanking God for the clarity of his word. "It's right out there in front of us and leaves us with no questions," she says.

Miller keeps the group on topic, making this class a clearer example than the one at Springs Community of Arthur's technique: a detailed, line-by-line explication of the text, with right and wrong answers. Before getting to details, though, they start, as Arthur instructs, by summarizing the three chapters.

"Why are gifts given to the body?" Miller asks.

"For edifying," comes one answer.

But that's not the answer she wants, and she keeps pushing. "How did they get into the body? How were the members placed in the body? How?"

Finally she gives up. "As God desires," she says. "They were placed in the body as God desires."

They move into a detailed discussion of gifts. "What about definitions? What did you learn when you looked at your definitions?"

Nobody wants to jump into this one. She keeps asking, squeezing the answers out of them word by word. What is a spiritual gift? Why does God give it? How does it show itself?

"I love the analogy of the body because it makes spiritual gifts clear," Miller says once she's gotten them through the passage. "There are teachings that say I am supposed to have the same gifts as others, but it ain't necessarily so."

Look at verse 29, she says. "'Are all apostles? Are all teachers?' What is the obvious answer?"

She gets a chorus of "no's".

"He makes it so clear," she says. "God's word is so clear."

"If the gifts were floating around without teaching," volunteers one class member, "we know what havoc there would be. Gifts need to operate under sound teaching."

They all know churches where that doesn't happen—charismatic churches that emphasize speaking in tongues. "Why do they emphasize one gift?" Miller asks.

"It's so obvious," is one answer, "and it brings praise."

"It draws attention," Miller says. "But if we were operating the way we should be, others would be—what?"

"Edified," they chant happily.

"They just ignore chapters 12 and 13," Miller says. "They've taken a piece of scripture from here and there and built a doctrine from that, and they think because of their showy gifts they are more spiritual."

The link to Paul, whose church at Corinth was doing exactly the same thing, seems inescapable, but nobody makes it. I don't think they've missed it; I think to them it's irrelevant. This is God's word written to them directly; what need have they to imagine their way into the life of a first-century church?

But as they plow through Paul's injunctions about when and how to use tongues, and the virtues of prophecy, I at least am missing something—or rather someone. I'm missing Paul. It is an achievement to read the letters of arguably the most vivid character in the New Testament without casting even a passing glance in his direction.

Instead, they sift through the passage looking for instructions. Miller has charted Paul's comparisons between tongues and prophecy on the board, but she can't make them match exactly. "I think he's talking about collective use of tongues," she says. "I don't mean to make this confusing."

It's hard, I think, *not* to be confusing when you're trying to systematize a thinker who developed his theology on the fly.

"If there is no interpreter, people who speak in tongues should keep silent in church," says one class member.

"But how do you know the interpretation is a true interpretation?" asks another.

"One test," says Miller, "would be, Would God say something like that? If you can't find it in scripture—"

"But a lot of interpretation is bland," objects one woman. "It's not unscriptural, but it's not coming from the heart."

"A lot of people are using preaching based not on scripture, but experience," says another. "And all experience is obviously not from the Lord."

Miller seems to be about to end the class when somebody raises the issue of Paul's teaching about women. Suddenly, First Corinthians becomes a book written by a particular, quite possibly fallible man.

"You can see it two ways," says Miller, floundering a bit. "He does say women should have their hair covered, but when you get to 14 . . . this chapter is a mess. I know there are traditions he had to deal with. There could have been a disorganized condition here, or women speaking in tongues."

"It doesn't say a woman shouldn't be a pastor," one class member notes.

"I have no problem," Miller responds, "with somebody telling me I have no business in the pulpit."

"But people use this scripture to beat women."

Time is up, Miller says. Kay's lecture is about to begin.

The auditorium—or at least the stage—is familiar from the tape I saw in Colorado. Miller busies herself urging the audience, which is 99 percent female, to fill up the front rows, and pitching leftover packages of books from a conference the previous weekend. "You all go buy them," she says, "because I don't want to take them apart." A dressed-up little boy of seven or eight comes out from the wings and recites a set of Bible verses, to enthusiastic applause. Arthur follows him out and gives him a big hug, then asks how her scarf looks on camera. "If you don't like it, I have an alternative."

"Try the alternative," says a voice from behind the camera. Arthur takes the scarf off.

Warming up the audience, she tells a story about a man who took her books into a Muslim country where he offered free tae kwan do lessons to anyone who did the Precepts courses. "Nineteen of them have received Christ and a twentieth is on the verge," she says. "Isn't it exciting to be able to pray for these things?"

"Ten, nine, eight . . ." comes the count from behind the camera, and Arthur steps forward, smiling earnestly. "A little knowledge can be a dangerous thing," she says. "The Corinthians needed milk because they hadn't grown up, yet we know they came behind in no spiritual gift. So now he is going to speak concerning spirituals, as the Greek says."

As she parses the Greek, the camera pans over the audience.

"Since they're zealous, he wants them to have a correct understanding," she says. "He wants them to bring their experience and feelings and thinking up against the truth of the word of God."

She speaks with authority. "The gifts are distributed according to God's will. You hear people say, 'Pray for this gift,' or 'All gifts are available to you.' But I think if you took every passage about gifts, you'd find that God gives the gifts and distributes them not according to your praying but according to his will. God doesn't speak out of one side of his mouth and then another. You have to look where the emphasis is put. Never take an obscure verse and use it to contradict what is spoken over and over. You can go after your own desires if you want, but you get leanness. You can continue to work in your own way, but it"—she breaks into song—"ain't necessarily so."

Miller had quoted the same song at the same point; this lecture is not as unrehearsed as it looks.

It's not exactly show time up there, but Arthur knows how to keep it moving. "Can you see my hands and my feet?" she asks, wiggling them. "You see some, but how my liver and intestines look? Nobody wants to see that. You see the seemly parts. But would you rather do without something seemly or your heart? You can live without an arm or a hand, but not without your liver."

Church services in those days were not like ours, she says. "When they came together, it was a very active, participating group, not one man standing lecturing, one group singing, and nothing from the audience but 'praise the Lord' and 'amen.' So he's telling you the rules in the service."

She tackles the troublesome question of women's role in church head-on. "Women are to keep silent—what does it mean? I think it means what it says. The context is tongues, and the word for 'speak' is the same word as in verse 28. I haven't always obeyed this. I have been asked to do church services, and I used to, but I don't anymore."

It's not an unambiguous teaching, she acknowledges. "The balance for me is 11:5," she says, referring to a verse in which Paul says women are not to pray or prophesy with uncovered head. "That's what makes the difference, because prophets aren't doing it at home, they're doing it in gatherings or in church. But you can get varieties of interpretation even in our staff. None of them want me to sit down and shut up. I think 'be subject' is the key. I am to be in submission. And I think in this church women had freedom and confidence and said, 'We'll do it our way.'"

She winds it up gracefully and right on time. "You can't deny experience," she says, "but use your head, and bring your experience under the discipline of the plumb line of the word of God."

I interview Arthur in front of an audience; about a dozen members of her staff are sitting with us at the big, round table in the dining room, watching and occasionally kibitzing. Her books are used, she tells me, in both conservative and liberal churches. "We've even been in a Mormon church. Some people are so conservative they would say we have no right being there. But we think, How will they know the truth if they don't know the word of God? John 17: 'thy word is truth.'"

The liberals I know wouldn't be comfortable with her teaching, I say. "They're wrong," she says, smiling to take some of the sting away. "When you look at Jesus, some believe he was the son of God, some believe he was a nice guy, some believe he's God in the flesh, but it doesn't alter who he is."

Who is he for you? I ask.

"He is God in the flesh. With the Father he has been from the beginning. He is the only way to God, and any man who does not know, embrace, and confess him will perish eternally.

"Of course," she adds, "if I am with people who don't believe, I am more polite about it.

"Look at Mark," she says, eager to prove her point. "Many of those people had religion but not a relationship. What Jesus Christ does is come into society and manifest himself for who he is. In John 10 he says he knows his sheep. Ten is connected to nine, where you have the man blind from birth. He is kicked out of the temple, a terrible thing for a Jew. Jesus says they are blind, but you can see. We are always blind. And I am used of God to show the light. I am just his spokesman."

A lot of what she does just teaches careful reading, I say. She nods agreement. "Not that different from teaching Shakespeare," I add, and she takes issue.

"Shakespeare isn't alive and powerful and sharper than a two-edged sword. It's the word of man, not the word of God. This [she points to a Bible] has the answer. It's the pure, unadulterated, absolute truth. All of us can tell stories of people who say, 'Because of learning this word, I made it. I have the power of life. I know where I'm going.'"

But she does use dramatic techniques in teaching, she says, citing biblical precedent. "Look at Ezekiel. The Lord said he should lie on his side. He used visuals." She had her students draw pictures of the book of Revelation, and when she taught the book recently on the Isle of Patmos, where it was written, she had the students act it out. "We had people playing the seals and trumpets and bowls, and then we pulled someone out of the crowd to be the dragon. God showed me how to do it on the cruise ship. My husband said, 'You're never going to do that,' but people said they finally had a grasp of Revelation."

She is looking in my eyes, with her hand on my arm, and has hardly even paused for breath. I am scribbling as fast as I can, and I can't get all of it.

She is telling me how the Holy Spirit guides her work. "I was at a meeting where they mentioned Hosea, and I turned to Hosea, where he talks about the wilderness, and the Holy Spirit went zing. I saw how it fits into the woman in the wilderness in Revelation. There's always something new the Holy Spirit will bring to mind to help us piece it together."

I ask whether she ever deals with questions of how the Bible was put together, the history of the individual books. "Events can be extraordinarily significant," she says, adding that there's an essay on the history of scripture in the *Inductive Study Bible*. "I want people to know how scripture was canonized."

Why doesn't she do a course on it? I ask. "My time has to be spent somewhere, and it's more valuable leading people to God. Daniel 11:32b: 'A people who know their God will be strong.' Our mission statement is to establish people in God's word."

It's hard to feel we've had a conversation—and I'm not sure Arthur thinks we have. "Please check whatever you want to quote with me," she says, "for accuracy and context." The request—as well as the crowd of admirers watching our interview—make me suspect that however active God may be in her work, she's not at all sure he's active in mine.

It would be easy to say I felt the same about her, but in fact my reaction was more complex. At one point, in the auditorium, I looked over at the open Bible in the lap of the woman sitting next to me. It was heavily marked, in a multitude of colors, and it was well worn.

Liberal Bible readers like to scoff that right-wing Christians don't actually read their Bibles; they just quote carefully selected texts. Jim Wallis, a radical evangelical preacher who has made a kind of one-man crusade of offering a biblical alternative to the Christian Coalition, used to boast that Ralph Reed wouldn't debate him because he knew Wallis could out-Bible him six ways from Sunday.

Perhaps that's true—of Reed. As a blanket statement about conservative Christians, it's palpably false. And people like Kay Arthur are one of the reasons. If you think the Bible matters, it's hard to wholeheartedly dislike somebody who teaches so many people to take it and read.

But what Arthur gives with one hand, she takes away with the other. To take her path into the Bible is to move down a road that narrows as you walk. When she says people have found life through her work, I have to believe her—I saw a bit of it myself. But her road to that life is a narrow one, and her entrance gate opens only to those with the right key.

Reconnoitering II

I t was a black man who worked for the Christian Coalition who first got me wondering whether I knew anything at all about conservative Christians. His name was Earl Jackson. He was a Boston minister with three jobs and half-a-dozen telephone numbers: a real operator, good-looking, friendly, intense, and ferociously right-wing.

I was writing a story for *Mother Jones* on the Christian Coalition's highly publicized but short-lived effort at racial reconciliation. Jackson was its point man, and for reasons never entirely clear to me, he agreed to let me follow him down to Mississippi, where he and a local black pastor, Lawrence Haygood, were meeting with local Christian Coalition members to try to get something going.

The Coalition members who came to the meeting were bursting with ignorance and good intentions, clearly troubled by the gulf between themselves and their black brothers and sisters in Christ, but without a clue what to do about it. If the two groups just prayed together, they hoped, it would go away. They were blind to the institutionalized racism experienced by every black person, liberal or conservative, in this country. It never crossed their minds that reaching across that gulf might force them to change.

But in all this, they weren't all that different from a lot of white liberals. Indeed, I've seen more people of color in the conservative churches I've visited than I have in most of the liberal ones. They were not stupid, these people, and certainly not evil. They knew something was wrong, and they were trying to take responsibility for making it right.

The day after the meeting, the two black pastors and I went for an all-day drive into deepest Mississippi. Memories of the old South ran deep in both men, who joked uneasily about what the cops would think of a car with two black men in the front seat and a white woman in the back. When Haygood pointed out the fields in which he'd picked cotton as a child, Jackson shuddered. "I don't want to hear about it," he said.

We talked a lot about the Bible. Early on, I mentioned how ironic it was that my childhood church (along with many others) used Genesis 31:49 as a blessing: "May the Lord watch between me and thee, while we are absent one from the other." In the context—the final parting between Jacob and his father-in-law Laban, who are anything but friends—it's not a blessing at all. It's a nonaggression pact. "May God keep us from killing each other" is a lot closer to what they're saying.

They turned in their seats to look at me, surprise in their faces. This liberal knew her Bible? It changed the whole tenor of the day. It didn't stop Jackson and me from arguing over everything from sex to scriptural authority, but it made it as much of a game as a war. I had the feeling he was pushing to see just how far I would go. And I, of course, was pushing back.

At one point he brought up the movie, *The Last Temptation of Christ*, which conservative Christians opposed bitterly. Weren't you shocked, he asked, at the idea of Jesus having sex? Not particularly, I said, but I couldn't believe *anybody* would follow someone as lugubrious as Scorcese's Jesus. He laughed in a kind of stunned way, and I wondered if this could be the first time he'd ever seen a redeeming value in irreverence.

He pursued the issue. Don't you believe that great art can only be created with the purpose of ennobling and inspiring us? No, I said, I believe great art is created for sheer delight in its creation.

As God created the world, I might have added, but I didn't think he'd buy the analogy. To him, as to most of the conservatives I've met, the world is not full of the grandeur of God. It is at war with God.

But it's not hard for me to understand why they feel that way. Jackson had a list of public-school horror stories: the day his fourth-grade daughter came home with a sexuality survey that asked how often she had wet dreams; the disdain that greeted his offer to give a talk about Christianity after the students had heard talks on wicca and astrology. For him, as for other conservatives, American culture feels like a threatening place: sex-obsessed, money-grubbing, and utterly out of control. Sometimes, like when I'm trashing my fifteenth unsolicited e-mail ad of the day for a sexy-teenager Web site, or watching a billboard truck proceed down Broadway, polluting at once the atmosphere and my visual space, I'm inclined to agree with them.

The black-and-whiteness of their views is harder to take. For me, discernment of God's will is an always-uncertain endeavor, a dance whose steps I will never, this side of heaven, completely master. For most of the conservatives I met, discernment is simply a matter of learning the rules, and then following them.

I don't get it.

Except that I do. There is a fundamentalist corner in me, after all, as there is in most liberals I know. We too seek the comfort of knowing precisely where the line is drawn between who's in and who's out, who's right and who's wrong, who's saved and who's damned. Often, in fact, our line is in exactly the same place where the conservatives have put it—we simply flip the picture over, putting ourselves inside and those other folks outside.

We human beings seem to need lines. After all, if there is no line, if there is no absolute, then there is nothing to trust except God's mercy. And compared to believing in God's mercy, believing in God is a piece of cake.

It is perhaps this reluctant fellow feeling that explains why I came away from my travels with a sneaking affection, and even admiration, for the conservatives I'd met. They cared about God, and studied his word, with a passion I only wished I could emulate. For them, knowing how to please God is a matter of ultimate importance, and if they can find out how to do that by reading the Bible, then they will read the book to tatters.

But behind that passion there lurks, I came to feel, an ugly shadow: the shadow of hell. Not that I heard about hell a lot. On the contrary, the people I met seemed obsessed by heaven. But, as Kathleen Boone, author of *The Bible Tells Them So,* a perceptive analysis of the workings of fundamentalism, told me when I called to talk to her about the conservative mind-set, one definition of heaven is that it's not hell.

"I'm not boggled by their obsession over whether or not they get into heaven," she said, when I told her that I was. "When you understand the concept of hell, you would have a compelling interest in getting into heaven. If people are being described by Jesus Christ himself as being in everlasting fire, how could you not be obsessed by that?"

It's confusing, nonetheless, because in so many ways the conservatives I met almost ignored Jesus. For them, the center of the New Testament seems to be not the Gospels, but the epistles: the letters, from Paul and others, about how to shape your church and live your life. It's not the stories they respond to, but the rules.

This came home most clearly to me when I listened to a bunch of conservative pastors explicate one of the greatest stories in all the Bible: the story of Joseph, sold by his brothers as a slave into Egypt, who becomes the de facto ruler of the country and the ultimate decider of his brothers' fate.

I first learned about BOLD (Business Outreach Lord Directed) when I attended a service at a Pentecostally oriented Presbyterian church in the outer reaches of Queens, an hour's subway ride from my house in Brooklyn. The pastor is one of BOLD's speakers, and a leaflet was lying on the table outside the auditorium where the church meets. The program offers half-hour lectures on the Bible at several New York area churches, given by a rolling collection of clergy.

I went, for the first time, to hear Tim Keller, a big star in New

York conservative Christian circles, whose East Side church draws yuppies in the hundreds. I went back again, several times, to try to figure out just why it was that the lectures—so sensible, so entertaining, so reasonable and realistic—left me feeling so queasy.

Keller had the audience in the palm of his hand as he talked about Joseph's troubles. "Joseph was downsized, stabbed in the back, in prison, sexually tempted, out of prison, working his way to the top—a typical New York City person," he said.

And what's more, I agreed with the message he drew from Joseph's story. "If you were to see a book titled *The Man God Uses*," he asked, "what would you assume? That it was a missionary, or somebody in the ministry. But Joseph, and Daniel, and Esther, got mightily used, and they weren't ministers. They weren't leading a church—they were taking their faith out into the professional world."

It's a lot simpler to be a minister, Keller said. "In church, you know what the rules are, but if you're a Christian in dance, or acting, or business, the rules are nowhere near as simple."

"Lord, it's so important that we do things right," said another speaker a few weeks later in his closing prayer. And that, I realized, was the problem. Keller, as well as the other BOLD speakers I heard, didn't seem to be so much responding to the Joseph story as mining it for moral lessons: don't get mad at God; don't hold grudges; take responsibility for your family. In the story as story, as an absorbing and, in the end, deeply moving account of the way people are, they took little interest.

But then, in the conservative mind-set, it's the way people are that is precisely the problem. Conservatives give lip service to the doctrine of the incarnation—the doctrine that in Jesus, God actually became a human being. But in fact, they rush past it so fast you can hardly see it for the dust. In their view, God's only motive for becoming human seems to have been to remove all traces of humanity from us as quickly as possible.

For all my sympathy with the conservatives, I could not live in the world they would create. At a National Day of Prayer service shortly after I arrived in Colorado Springs, one of the prayer leaders called on Jesus to seize control of the airwaves. "Not your Jesus," was all I could think. It was clear from the way he addressed him that his Jesus would replace parables with morality tales, ambiguity with certainty, and story with dogma.

"How arrogant," said my sister when she read the newspaper article about Haggard's World Prayer Center, "to believe you know what God wants." When I quoted her remark to Haggard, he laughed. "Conservatives," he said, "aren't afraid to know what they know."

He had a point. In their eagerness not to offend anybody at all, liberals often seem terminally wishy-washy. But . . . "you know what I miss out here?" I responded. "I miss mystery."

"You're right," he said. "We don't do mystery very well."

The reader-response theorists I met at the Society for Biblical Literature convention sometimes seemed to be saying that the Bible means anything anybody wants it to—in other words, nothing at all. But they recognize something the conservatives seem to miss entirely—that the reader and the Bible enrich each other; that this is a cooperative venture. For conservatives, the Bible is a book of commands that leaves the reader only one choice: to follow or not to follow. Their Bible, like the world they would make in its image, has no shading, and no color.

When Kay Arthur teaches that the Bible is clear and consistent, or when Jim Tomberlin tells me it's a user-friendly operator's manual, they are stripping the book of everything that, for me, gives it power. A God who is easy to understand, who wants only obedience, who hands out rewards and punishments like some particularly efficient chief executive, is for me no God at all.

But for all that, I can't help also realizing that conservatives know something about the Bible that most of the liberals I know have forgotten: that it speaks, in the most intimate and ultimate way, of life and death.

Whenever Peter Gomes watches one of the perennial undergraduate arguments over the nature of God, he told me, he knows who's going to win. "The liberal goes down to crashing defeat because he hasn't become acquainted with the central book of his tradition. Either he's converted on the spot, or he drops out entirely.

"Admiring literature won't get you into heaven," he said. "What clicks in these nonliterate traditions about the Bible is not intellectual or esthetic. It's a transforming experience. If you come to the Bible thinking it's an interesting book and you want to know more about it, you get what you can and away you go. But if your assumption is that this book is not like any other, that in this book God is talking to you in ways that are essential for you to understand, then you ask how you are going to enter into it."

That was the question with which the conservatives left me. Can I, without buying their interpretation, find in the Bible the voice of God that it is essential for *me* to understand? Is there a way for those of us to whom the Bible cannot speak literal truth to enter into it with the same passion and commitment?

Chapter 10

Artists

Roanoke, VA; New York City; Patchogue, NY; Northern California

It is a balmy December morning—and a good thing, too, because the only place to sit outside the Bronwyn Keenan Gallery is an iron staircase. The building—an old warehouse on New York's Lower East Side—is locked, and nobody is answering the bell.

The gallery is showing an art exhibit I'm eager to see. The novelist Darcey Steinke has put together a show of what the *New York Times* (sounding a bit bemused) called "religiously influenced art." I've been curious about how artists read the Bible, and I figure this is one way of finding out.

The pictures, once I get inside to see them, aren't at all what I'd expected. The *Times* article reproduced one of the most overtly religious pieces in the collection: a dramatic canvas by the Rev. Ethan Acres. Against a fiery sky, an androgynous figure in biblical flowing robes is holding a bedroll and a sign saying "Will work for food" in one arm; the other holds out a floppy hand puppet that looks more like a cow than anything else. In the foreground, a figure that's clearly Acres, dressed in black and holding a Bible, has fallen to the ground in a pose reminiscent of pictures of the conversion of St. Paul. Acres told the *Times* that the picture represents a dream in which God appeared to him in the guise of a homeless person holding a hand puppet.

There are, of course, other religious, and even biblical, images here. One of the biggest paintings in the room, William Rutherfo-ord's *The Church of What's Happening Now,* is a bleakly hostile portrait of a snake handler surrounded by rats and weasels (see Mark 16:18). *Give Me That Old Time Religion,* by Joe Coleman, piles on Roman Catholic iconography with the abandon, and fury, of Hieronymus Bosch; his Virgin looks like an Anne Rice vampire.

But there's a lot here whose connection with religion seems pretty tenuous. There are pink-and-blue photo montages of clouds and lambs and naked women, and a lovely stained-glass portrayal of a man and a woman in what seems to be a cave or a bunker. One photograph, by Andres Serrano, shows a corpse in the morgue; another, by Max Aguilera-Hellweg, a human heart in a doctor's gloved hand.

"You know what," I said to the artist friend who'd come with me, "they've all got an attitude." That's contemporary art for you, he replied. "It's all about the artist."

And that's the way she wanted it, Steinke told me when I talked to her about the show. Traditional religious paintings put the story first and the artist second. "They were more like illus-trations: more upfront, with less subterfuge."

The contemporary art world—and Steinke herself, for that matter—wants to see the artist's own attitude clearly reflected in the work. "You couldn't be considered a serious artist and just do biblical paintings," she said. "If I go to see an art show that I hear has religious overtones, and then it's all painted biblical depic-tions, I'm disappointed. This is the twentieth century. I want to see how current issues and struggles for faith are intersecting." Steinke has done much the same thing in print; she and novelist Rick Moody recently edited a book of essays by contemporary writers that took the Bible as a springboard.

"I like it when artists do everything new, with no signs and sig-nifiers from anything else," she told me. "I didn't want any depic-tions of Jesus in my show—it turns so many people off. People come with so much in the way of prescribed ideas and values. They never read the New Testament; they feel they've been abused by faith; they don't like fundamentalists; but they have a Christian sensibility. That's what my show is about—Christian sensibility, and the way it overlaps and where the resonance is."

I left the exhibit feeling I'd learned more about contemporary art than about how artists read the Bible. Perhaps hearing my frustration in my questions, Steinke suggested I talk to Bill Rutherfoord. The snake handler, she told me, was not typical of his work. "He's done the stations of the cross, and altars," she said, "and he's suffered a lot in the art world for the kind of work he does."

The snake-handler painting was in fact an attack on fundamentalism, Rutherfoord told me. "It's about the hazards of literal interpretations of religious texts. The whole snake-handler culture is based on a literal reading of one line in Mark's gospel. That's a complete subversion."

The picture is also part of a series representing the four horsemen of the Apocalypse; the snake handler is the white horseman. When I said I'd missed that, Rutherfoord wasn't surprised—the reference to Revelation is in code. In a code of a code, in fact. Superimposed on the snake handler's belt buckle is a tiny copy of a strange and famous image in Holbein's *The Ambassadors*. Viewed straight on, the image looks like nothing at all, but viewed from the side, it's clearly a skull.

"In the opinion of many people I've talked to, *The Ambassadors* is actually an apocalyptic painting," Rutherfoord told me. "When you start looking at it, the objects on the table behind the two men are all about the end time. There's a stringed instrument, for instance, with a broken string, which can be interpreted as a reference to the world being out of tune. During the Reformation, when the picture was painted, people were convinced that the world was coming asunder and the apocalypse was at hand."

The whole Apocalypse series is crowded with similar references, he told me. The first in the series, which precedes the four horsemen, pictures what look like seven Klansmen. But they're not. They're actually Spanish *penitentes,* and they represent the seven churches to whom the book of Revelation is addressed. They also serve—along with a crow that's also in the picture—as a reference to the famous Eisenheim altar piece. "There are holy cards around the necks of the *penitentes,*" Rutherfoord told me. "One is Anthony Abbot, and one is Paul the Hermit. An art historian will recognize that those are from Eisenheim and will then make a leap to the crow. And from that he will conclude that the painting is saying something about being removed from the broader community of the church and pursuing a perhaps eccentric view of Christianity." The hermit, he explained, represents isolated monasticism, while the abbot stands for the organization of monks into groups.

For Rutherfoord, the two figures also speak of his own position in the art world—on the fringes. "If you're an artist, and look at the monastic model, it's easy to find yourself in one of those positions. If you're in New York, you're part of the group, but if you're out here where I am, you're on your own." The churches in Asia Minor to whom the book of Revelation was addressed were also outside what was becoming the Christian mainstream, he said. "What I'm driving at here is that perhaps what is perceived as the Gnostic heresy may not be as wrongheaded as orthodoxy considers it."

Intellectually complex as his paintings are, Rutherfoord said they come out of a direct interaction with biblical texts and with church history. He cited a crucifix he'd done—part of a series called *The Blighted Chapel*—in which the cross on which Jesus is crucified is a tree. "There's a psalm that talks of the beams of the temple being hewn apart, and that image is useful in the broader sweep of church history. You can see the Reformation as a kind of tearing down of the temple and a re-forming of it. The tree is the central roof beam of the temple, and there is a tradition that Christ was crucified on a cross made from a beam of the temple. Then in the main part of the crucifix there's a great fire, and you can make out architectural elements, including a steeple whose cross intersects the arm of the crucifix. That's a further development of the tearing down of the old corrupt framework."

I asked whether he figures all this out before starting a picture. "I may have a broad idea at the outset about how this work is going to shape out," he said, "but if one of my original notions seems wrong for it, I won't use it. I'll do something else. It's very Ignatian. The process determines what's going to happen next."

Until he mentioned Ignatius, I had been finding Rutherfoord's explanations, clear though they were, hard to grasp. My mind works verbally much more than visually; ideas, for me, naturally express themselves in words. With Rutherfoord's pictures in front of me, I couldn't deny the subtlety of his thought process, but I was having a hard time imagining my way out of words and into images.

With Ignatius, though, I was on familiar ground. Ignatius had changed my life.

I first discovered Ignatian prayer in somewhat the same circumstances that Ignatius himself developed it in the sixteenth century—when I was sick as a dog. Ignatius, wounded in battle as a young man, whiled away a long and painful recovery by reading everything he could get his hands on—everything from romances to religious classics. In the process, he discovered the power of his imagination, which could create vivid pictures, spawned by his reading, of everything from wooing a fair lady to dying for Christ. But what he also discovered was that these different fantasies had different results. When he imagined doing great feats to win a lover, he was filled with joy, but joy that disappeared quickly. But when he imagined himself passionately following God, the joy remained, and grew stronger, when the fantasy ended.

The result of this discovery was *The Spiritual Exercises,* one of the few methods of prayer that uses the imagination as a friend instead of an enemy. Picture in your imagination a scene from scripture, Ignatius taught. Place yourself in the scene, and then go wherever God and your imagination take you.

This is not an easy thing for most of us intellectual folk to do. We're fine *thinking* about the Bible, but when we try to picture it, to set a scene going in our heads, we feel silly and artificial. Our mental store of biblical images has in any case been poisoned by Hollywood; just try imagining Moses on the mountain without thinking of Charlton Heston. "I can't get anything but Jesus movies," sighed one friend after his first try.

I am no different, but I was lucky—pushed over the hump by a high fever and a mild delirium that destroyed my inhibitions. In that state, I had only to read a story out of the Bible and it would unroll itself in front of me, going places I never would have expected it to go. The process, independent of any conscious control, was at once simple, astonishing, and wildly entertaining.

Once I got well, of course, my intellect reasserted itself and it got harder. I became conscious of the complex interplay between thought, feeling, and imagination, and it became, as it still is, a struggle to let the prayer have its own way. But when it does, it brings me as close to the experience of the great creative artist as I suspect I will ever come. Whether you want to call it God, or creativity, or the flow, the power working through me brings ideas and understandings that first amaze and then slowly reshape my prosaic, everyday self. As Rutherfoord said, it is the process itself that creates the outcome.

Simon Carr, who accompanied me to Steinke's exhibit, is also a religious artist, but a very different one from Rutherfoord. Carr's work shifted from abstract to narrative once he became a Christian; for him, to paint the scene is to tell the story as clearly as he can. So I was amused to find, when I visited his studio— crammed not only with his own paintings but a wild assortment of religious images—that he, too, takes Ignatius as a model. "If you know *The Spiritual Exercises,* that's the whole plot," he told me—"the idea that a painting is a loaded experience, that the painter is constructing a situation that someone is going to project themselves into to reach a personal resolution."

Carr was inveigled into Christianity through his children, students at St. Luke's School in Greenwich Village. "The kids were mad about church from the beginning, but I was like a wolf on the edge of the firelight. I said church was fine, but you weren't going to catch *me* at a service."

The decision to be baptized came slowly and in many ways

reluctantly. But once it happened, he said, "it changed every-thing about the way I understood my life. There's an image of Donne's, that sin is like a harpooner. Well, this was like a Nan-tucket sleigh ride. On the one hand, it was terrifying. But on the other hand, I'd trained my whole life to have my hands ready for this."

The first change in his painting was that his abstracts became more like Greek crosses. One day a consultant for a major Wall Street bank, which had bought a lot of his work, called with a question about the new stuff. "They asked if these were religious paintings," he told me, grinning. "I said it depends on your point of view—but I knew I was lying. There was a secret text."

Now, Carr paints almost nothing but biblical scenes. "I've got-ten so involved in this incarnation thing, this flesh thing," he said to me. "Christianity is a religion of narrative. Jesus came as a fig-ure in space, a three-dimensional, Hellenistic form. And the Bible is the most stunning text to work from, narratively, because it constructs, visually, situations that are so full of emotional intensity and power."

It was the Gospel of John that pushed him into narrative, he said. "When I did the raising of Lazarus, I knew I had to come back to figures. When Christ is approaching the cave, and Lazarus is wrapped up—it's very rare that you get such a vivid visual. It projects you into the scene to the point where you can experience it, and that's what I'm trying to do—to make my expe-rience and my investigating an entrance point for viewers to con-duct their own interest and exploration and resolution.

"The greatest thing I can be," he went on, "is a window. I hope my paintings will discuss issues that quickly become the point of looking at them. That's not a very twentieth-century idea of what an image is for, but I'm very comfortable with the idea that my ego, enormous as it is, will get left behind."

Carr's studio is full of reproductions of earlier artists' takes on his subjects, and he has little patience with the twentieth-century desire for art that's completely new. "Any painter who thinks he's working outside the museum is fooling himself," he said flatly. "I've seen people stand on their heads to do it, and they might as well cut their hands off. I love the tradition deeply. I'm real glad to be a union member. When I look at a Van Dyck sketch when I'm doing Mary Magdalene, I want to break my brushes on it. My task is to throw myself at the tradition and watch myself go down in flames."

Unlike Rutherfoord's, Carr's paintings are simple: big blocks of color in which the story, not the iconography, takes precedence. One of his paintings, for instance, is based on a brief reference, in the book of Acts, to sick people lying where Peter's shadow would pass over them and heal them. There are no sick people in Carr's painting—but there is nonetheless a narrative. Peter, in a blue robe, stands in an almost empty landscape: orange earth and a paler orange sky divided only by the blue line of the lake of Galilee, boats and fishermen barely visible at its edge. Peter, with his hands lifted in front of him as though he is praying, or arguing, is staring at the shadow at his feet, whose shape could be that of a crucified man. What he sees in it is mysterious, but the picture is charged with tension.

"I hear these stories, and they construct and conflate and work their way around and change," Carr said. "I never really have to search for one because they're so busy pursuing me. I read chapter 21 of John and I see a yellow sky, and I could paint it till I drop. If I wasn't painting them, they'd be prayers."

When we talked, Carr was working on a commission—a painting of Jacob's ladder—and he told me a bit about how he was going at it. "It's never the way, to look, and then imagine, and then paint," he said. "I go back and forth between the text and the picture, and my understanding of the text changes dramatically as my thinking changes." Carr, a faithful member of St. Luke's Bible study group, gets irritable at what he calls "this whole thing about painters being dumb." He analyzes scripture as carefully for his paintings as he does in Bible study; he based one character in the Jacob painting on a variant reading of the Hebrew.

Jacob, which was not yet finished when we talked, had already been changed hundreds of times. "A lot of times when I paint a gesture, it's not that I think of it and then do it, but I paint it and then recognize it: 'Of course, that's what Jacob's saying.' I don't go in knowing and painting what I know. I go in not knowing much and then discover what I know."

The Bible has never dominated Western literature in quite the way that, for centuries, it dominated Western art. To visit an art museum without some familiarity with the biblical story is to walk through a lot of the galleries almost blind. For a reader, though, especially a reader of prose, the biblical connections are less overt. At least until this century, Western novels resonated with biblical language and images, but in most cases you didn't need a Bible to understand the plot or the characters.

Poets, though, have been as taken with the biblical stories as painters—perhaps more so. Unlike painters, they weren't usually being paid by the church; most of them could pick their subjects to please themselves, so if they used the Bible, it was because they wanted to, something that, with painters, you can't always be sure of. To get at least a glimpse of how the poetic imagination tackles scripture, I went out to Long Island to talk to Laurance Wieder, who—in addition to being a poet himself—chose most of the poems in *Chapters into Verse,* a two-volume Bible told not in the original text, but in the words of hundreds of poets, from George Herbert and Walt Whitman to Delmore Schwartz and Sylvia Plath.

Wieder had become bored with lyric poetry by the time he started working on *Chapters into Verse,* he told me. "One of the problems is that at some point the subject of lyric poetry is always oneself, and at some point that no longer seemed an interesting thing to write about." So he started writing in other voices: John Wayne, in *Duke: the Poems as Told to Laurance Wieder,* and the biblical psalmist, in *The Psalms.*

"Writing the psalms was an opportunity for me to find out for myself what I thought when confronted with what the text was," he said. "On the one hand, it's my voice, but the me is not me. One of the great things about the Psalms is that the 'I' is non-specific. John Donne said if you want to know what it means to be human, strip yourself of your name, place in life, date of birth, parents, possessions, citizenship. Take all of those away, and what is left is what it is to be human. The 'I' of the Psalms comes accoutered with a history, rank, and set of achievements, but somehow the voice that speaks out of that is not burdened by it."

When I asked Wieder what he'd learned from doing *Chapters into Verse* about how other poets read the Bible, he talked not about technique, or understanding, but about authority and love. After three years of immersion in poets' biblical interpretations, he came out convinced, he told me, that beauty is not the ultimate goal. "I think truth is what it's about, and it's not that what's beautiful is true or what's true is beautiful. Truth possesses a power that you can't gainsay. I never worked on *Chapters into Verse* that I didn't feel better when I was done.

"The difference between a meaningful reading and one that is shallow," he went on, "is that one has to acknowledge that oneself is not the measure of things; that there is something out there that is bigger than oneself, whatever it may be and whatever you may call it. That's what this book is, the story of that otherness. One of the fundamental distinctions in the Old Testament is between the Jews and the others. You can look at it as election or just think of it as a recognition of differences, but it isn't all one self, one version, one thing, one kind of experience."

Our culture suffers from a hostility towards the imagination that cuts across political lines, he said. "And it becomes even starker when it refers to this realm. I can say I talk to John Wayne and write down the conversation, and it doesn't bother anyone; but if I were to describe, as Blake does, my conversations with Isaiah and Ezekiel, people don't know what to make of it. The assertion of the imagination is that the accustomed world, the received world, is not the only world. But when you get Blake, who is obviously no fool, saying—on paper so you can't see if he's smiling—that I had dinner with Isaiah and Ezekiel, what do you do?"

Delight in it, he said. "For me, the delight is all the reason there needs to be."

What you don't do, he went on, is try to make it reasonable. "If you deal with it on the level of things to be reconciled and balanced, all you're doing is performing a task for yourself. It's a way of dismissing it. But if you say, 'No, this is something other than me, and my task is to figure out, in some way that convinces me, what it says,' then you've engaged the other. And that's also a definition of love."

One of Wieder's favorite passages in the Old Testament is Moses' words to the people of Israel before his death. "He says, 'I set before you life and good, and death and evil, that you may see them and know. And this is no vain thing for you, because it is your life.'" That's why we read the Bible, he says. "The reason isn't heaven or hell, or to become rich and famous, or get a theme park named after you. The reason is, it's your life. And if your life is a vain thing, then that's your problem."

I don't know whether every poet who reads it sees the Bible in such stark terms. But a few years ago, when our parish Bible study group was reading Stephen Mitchell's translation of Job, I talked briefly with Mitchell, a renowned writer and translator.

"I became interested in Job not as literature, but as a kind of Zen koan," he told me. "In my early twenties, when I was going through a very difficult experience, I felt powerfully attracted to the Book of Job." He was particularly struck, he said, by the Voice from the Whirlwind, God's long, gorgeously written but theologically problematic speech at the end of the book. As a response to Job's plaints, the speech has infuriated many readers. "Most people read the speech as saying, essentially, 'I know better than you, so shut up and accept,'" Mitchell said. "It's the ultimate put-down."

But the speech hit Mitchell very differently. "I knew instinctively that the poet had seen into reality. There was a genuine vision about human suffering and evil that I desperately needed to understand. The speech had a luminescence about it, which was happening beneath the surface of the words. I never found anyone besides William Blake who had a sense of what kind of answer the Voice from the Whirlwind might be, but for me, that answer was magnetic. It drew me to learning Hebrew, for starters, and learning textual scholarship—in order to be intimate with that vision."

After six years, though, he gave up. "I finally realized that I wasn't going to enter that place from words on a page, however magnificent and profound. And at that point life handed me a Zen master. After a year of intensive Zen practice, during a seven-day retreat, I suddenly found myself in the center of Job's whirlwind. The whole question of human suffering was brilliantly clear. Actually, the question had disappeared. I had become the answer." After that, Mitchell could come back to the book and recognize what it was that drew him to it in the first place.

I originally decided to talk to artists about the Bible because I thought that their work might form a meeting place between liberals and conservatives. After all, I reasoned, parents of all stripes read C. S. Lewis's Narnia books (the first of which is an unmistakable retelling of the Christ story) to their children.

Five minutes into my conversation with Steinke, I realized what a naive notion that was. Artists' works and opinions, and the opinions of just about everybody else about those works and opinions, are as divided, as self-righteous, as stubbornly narrow, as any biblical discussion.

But though artists may not offer a meeting ground, I came away from my conversations believing that they can, perhaps, offer a way to some kind of common ground, a path by which liberals can find their own way to as passionate a relationship with the Bible as that of the conservatives.

All the artists I talked to would classify as biblical liberals— that is, they understand the Bible to be a human product and subject to error. None of them, as far as I could tell, looks to it as a road map to heaven or a guide to daily behavior.

But one thing they do share with conservatives: the Bible is, for them, a life-or-death matter. More than any of the scholars I met, it was the artists who were able to articulate for me the authority, the power, and the truth of this book.

I suppose, actually, that stands to reason. Scholars, and those of us who have been so deeply influenced by them, may talk about truth as something beyond mere fact. But neither they nor we are able to do a very good job of acting that out. Our world is so permeated with the importance of fact that it's hard for us to imagine any other way of looking at reality.

Artists don't think that way. For them, truth is not what we have been convinced of, but that which convinces. Carr knows he has painted the right gesture, not because he has figured out how Jacob would move, but because the gesture itself convinces him of its rightness. Truth, for Carr and the other artists I talked to, is not so much a matter of knowledge, or understanding, as of recognition—like seeing, across a room, a long-absent friend whom you had almost forgotten.

For the artists who have found that truth in the Bible, the book is anything but vain; they may not take it literally, but they know that it is, in the most literal sense, their life.

Chapter 11

First A.M.E. Church

Atlanta, GA

T he choir, in bright robes, is singing "Lift Me Higher,"
accompanied by choruses of "yes" from the congregation.
"You *will* praise him; you *will* praise him; he has worked *wonders*
for you," proclaims a grinning woman in a black cassock.

"Where God guides, God provides," is the motto of First
African Methodist Episcopal Church in Atlanta, a three-
hundred-member church that recently moved from a ghetto to a
more upwardly mobile black neighborhood. "On the other side
of town, nothing had been built new since 1954," pastor Earl
McCloud told me, explaining the move. "Over here, we have one
hundred thousand new houses. We have twenty-three boys in
our scouting program here, and there we could never get six. But
we're still trying to establish a new personality, and it has not
been easy." The church bought its building from a black Baptist
church that had been there twenty-one years. "They were
ingrained in this community." First A.M.E. has a bunch of social
activities—men's groups, women's groups, a book club, trips—
as well as prison ministries, a food pantry, and a computer lab.
This is the first southern black church I've spent time at, and the
biggest surprise for me is the formality. McCloud addresses all
his parishioners as Mr. or Mrs., and though I've quickly gotten

179

onto first-name terms with the other people I've talked to, I am hesitant to do so with him.

We've been doing church now for close to an hour, and we're nowhere near done. "Thank you Lord," come the shouts from the pews when the choir sits.

McCloud preaches on chapter 8 of Paul's second letter to the Corinthians, where he's asking them to contribute to the needs of poor Christians in Jerusalem. Paul is manipulating the Corinthians, McCloud says, telling them how much the poverty-stricken Macedonians have given to push the rich Corinthians to give even more.

"Paul is surprised at the Macedonians' level of giving. He says we saw it with our own eyes, nobody had to urge them. They volunteered to cut grass; they sold baked goods; they gave so much he didn't understand how they did it."

He moves seamlessly between Paul's words and the lives of his own congregation. "The Macedonian church had a lot going on; they were undergoing severe trials, but they experienced overflowing joy, extraordinary power. We know times will be hard, but we have survived hard times for a long time. We've survived hard times when there were no times but hard times. We're first cousin to hard times."

Where did the Macedonians get so much? They gave themselves first to the Lord, he says. "If you live with what you have, and not how much God has and what God can do with what you have, you're not there yet," he says. "If you're sick today and hurting tomorrow and dodging the bill collector, you're not there yet."

He's getting into the swing of it, and so is his congregation, which is urging him on with shouts and amens. "Give your heart and soul and mind and home and car and church and backaches and headaches and arthritis to the Lord—and he'll work it out. You may have an outdoor toilet, no TV, no remote control—but if you turn it over to the Lord, he'll work it out. God has a reputation for working things out."

At the announcements, McCloud gives a pitch for an alternative gas company that's contributing fifty dollars to the church for every parishioner that signs up with them. And he tells his people to get out and vote. "Call ten people and ask them to vote—we'll take them to the polls. Too many people bled and died for us to vote, for us not to vote. If we let the Republicans get any more hold than they have, we'll go further and further down."

McCloud teaches a couple of Bible studies a week, and I came back a few days later to watch. It's a truism among whites that black folk know their Bible; that when African Americans read the story of God leading the Israelites to freedom, they see in it their own story and their own hope. But the picture's a lot more complicated than that, McCloud tells me. Biblical literacy is threatened among blacks as well as among whites; a lot of his parishioners don't know the Bible at all. "I have to start with basic definitions and introduce it gradually." Not until they have some familiarity with the Bible can he start digging into what it is actually saying.

"For black people, the Bible has been a literal document," he told me; anything in the Bible came direct from the mouth of God. When he talks about the Macedonians and their bake sales, he's trying to counter that. "I'm trying to make people see that there are people like them in the Bible. If they can identify with somebody in the Bible, and they think the Bible is good, they see themselves as good.

"The people who come here are rarely interested in academics," he said. "I'd have a whole different conversation with you than I would with them. My real challenge is to make this book understandable for them. They don't care if God or Jesus is a man or a woman, so I don't raise it; they don't care if man was created first. I may point out that there are in fact two flood stories, but they don't care what's in the priestly tradition.

"You have to be able to pick out what is valuable," he said, citing Paul. To McCloud, Paul is a bigot. "But there's one piece which is so valuable, when he goes to God about the thorn in his side. Every person in this world has had a thorn in their side. I think that's a great piece of scripture."

I told McCloud about Kay Arthur's insistence on Paul's uniformity, and he hooted. "You can't make Paul consistent," he said. It's an approach he's been battling at First A.M.E. "When I first said to people here that most of the Psalms are not the word of God, they're utterances of people . . . you have to teach very carefully that these are human beings here."

By teaching his people to delve into the Bible, McCloud hopes to keep them from swallowing every statement in it wholesale. He told me a story originally told by black theologian Howard Thurman, who as a child read the Bible to his grandmother. "When he got to 'slaves, obey your masters,' she would say, 'Stop—my God ain't like that, and my God wouldn't say that.' But when you do an in-depth study, the passage also says, 'masters, treat your slaves in such a way that they won't rebel,' just as it tells husbands to treat wives in a way that deserves respect."

McCloud's noon Bible study is an introduction to the Old Testament, and they're working on Exodus. As in any daytime Bible study, the half-dozen here consists almost entirely of women. McCloud is drawing a spiral on the board, which he tells us is Mt. Sinai.

"The people of Israel came out of Egypt and wandered around in the desert and ended up here, for biblical studies' purposes, from Exodus 19 through Leviticus to Numbers 10. So when you come to the book of Deuteronomy, and the Lord says you've been around the mountain long enough, you see what he means."

Someone asks how long, precisely. "It's questionable, but if I had to guess, probably about two years."

He talks about the law given on Sinai. "One thing they learned from the law was what God was like. I am a jealous God. What makes a man jealous?—oh, Lord, don't answer that," he says quickly, remembering that he's talking to women. "What makes a woman jealous?"

"Competition from the opposite sex," says one.

"Well, the same kind of thing makes God jealous. If he faces competition from your leaning towards another god, God makes it clear that makes him jealous, and if God gets jealous, you ain't going to like what he's going to do."

God tells them how he expects them to live, he says—"and

that's a big one. When somebody starts telling you how to live, they're really beginning to get in your business."

He moves on to the point where a lot of readers give up: God's detailed, not to say tedious, instructions to Moses on just how to build the tabernacle. "He even tells him where to place the oil and the lamp stand," McCloud says. "He talks about blue and purple and scarlet yarns. God is not a general God; God builds in detail. But a lot of time the details don't come like we want them to come. For four hundred years, from the time he told him to build this stupid wooden thing, God didn't say anything to Noah, and I bet he could have used some hints. When I was praying about moving this church, God didn't say, 'McCloud, you're doing the right thing.' But instead of making one loan available, God made three."

This whole section is talking about obedience, McCloud says. "Remember in Second Kings where the woman's husband dies? She has nothing but two boys, and the bill collector is coming to collect the two boys and sell them as slaves. So she goes to Elisha, and says, 'My lord's servant, my husband, is now dead.' He tells her to pour a little oil, and she starts pouring, and it keeps coming. He tells her to go and sell the oil and pay off her debts. The important thing about the whole story is the woman's obedience. So, beloved, one of the things they learned from their time around the mountain was to trust God."

McCloud has been spending a good deal of time teaching his congregation about worship, and he grabs the chance to emphasize it here. "When you come into the presence of God," he says, "just the power of that presence consumes who you are."

"When I was a young woman in the A.M.E., they worshiped like Baptists and Pentecostals," says one woman. "Then they went through a period where they were worshiping like Anglicans. Now we are coming back to prayer and praise."

"Makes you happy, doesn't it?" asks McCloud.

"Oh, it sure does. The song and the praise and the testimony—it brings me back where I need to be. It's like a renewal and a refreshing station. It lifts my spirit."

"When you come in, if you start out singing 'Praise God from whom all blessings flow,'" says McCloud, "God lives inside of you and you are thankful just to make it to Sunday. Moses was just thankful to have arrived at this place. When Exodus begins, it begins in gloom, but when it goes out, Lord have mercy, it goes out in glory."

He begins introducing Leviticus. "When they come out of Exodus, the people have a place to worship, so the next book is almost a given. If they are going to have a place to worship, they have got to know how to worship, and Leviticus is a book that gives many, many, *many* instructions on how to worship. But there's a key verse: 19:2—'Be holy, because I the Lord am holy.' Lord have mercy. Be holy, Mrs. Pearson, because the Lord wants you to be holy, and you ain't going to do that, are you?'"

"I don't know," says Mrs. Pearson, looking a bit alarmed, "but I'm going to try."

"We are a living example of 'in our trying, we fail,'" McCloud responds.

He seems to me to be trying to dance a complicated minuet, both demonstrating the absoluteness of God's demands and giving his hearers permission to take issue with them. "I thought that was rather selfish of God," he had said earlier, of God's refusal to allow Moses into the tabernacle he had just finished building.

In an intellectual environment, the problem would probably be solved with an explanation that the instructions in Exodus and Leviticus are more likely to have been written by the priestly caste than by God. McCloud may himself reject that explanation—he told me that he was taught in seminary that Moses wrote the first five books of the Bible and for all I know that's what he still believes. Whatever his belief, though, I find myself admiring his refusal to take that simple route. Instead, he's opening doors for human response and reaction in what would otherwise be an intolerable and incomprehensible collection of "Thou shalt's." It's a tricky job.

He runs quickly through the major themes of Leviticus: worshiping a holy God and living a holy life. "We're going to try to get through about eight chapters at a time," he says. "Any questions about Exodus?"

"I was baffled in chapter 22," says one woman, "about a thief being caught. If it's nighttime and you struck him and he dies, you're not guilty, but if it's after sunrise, you're guilty."

"What I got," says another woman, "is that in daytime you can see, so you can defend yourself in some other way than killing him, but at night, you don't know if he's going to kill you first."

This is not alien material, it turns out; living, as many of them do, in dangerous neighborhoods, they are well versed in the legalities of self-protection.

Laura Walton, who figured out that puzzle in Exodus, has studied the Bible in many churches, but she says she's new at "serious Bible study." Most of what she got was anything but, she told me. "In one church, you would have different members of the class trying to teach, and they didn't know any more than I did. Other places, preachers would just teach the sections they wanted to espouse."

Walton grew up in a hellfire-and-damnation church, where makeup—and a lot more—were forbidden, but it didn't take. "My parents insisted we go, but they didn't beat us over the head with it," she said. "Then as I got older, and could read more and understand it for myself, I knew God wanted us to be as pretty as we can. He made the universe and put in flowers and trees, and we are to take our pattern after that.

"I'm just sore when I have to miss Bible study," Walton says. "Preachers can't take enough time in a sermon. But in Bible study you get a chance to express your opinion and hear others' opinions, and come to a conclusion—'Oh, I see your point,' or 'You're right,' or 'I didn't think about that.'"

Between her independence of mind and the give and take of Bible study, Walton has come to take a nuanced approach to scripture. "I do believe the Bible is the word of God," she said. "Everything in there that God said he would do, he is going to do. He told Moses to split the rock and he split the rock—that's how specific he is. When he gives instructions for building the ark, if he's that specific about how he wants his robe, then he's that specific when he tells of sin. You will be punished, and the punishment will be thus and so.

"But," she added, "I think it speaks to specific situations. If we are going for healing, you are going for one thing, and I another. I'm not sure if he intended for all of us to get the same measure. Two people could have two different interpretations, and God could be speaking through both. The Bible is an enigma. It takes a lot of depth and understanding."

"I want to try to create an argument tonight." McCloud had promised me fireworks at this study of First Corinthians, and now he is following through. About a dozen people, including several men this time, have gathered in the basement room. Some have brought their kids, who are running around the halls.

"There are some very male chauvinist things in the book of Corinthians," McCloud says. "Once we read it, we're going to divide up into two groups. I want us to have a dialogue about women and their roles and places." He sends the women over to the other side of the room, and gathers the men to him.

McCloud's tongue is firmly in his cheek, and his audience knows it. "From all my years of reading," he says solemnly to the women, "I have finally cleared it up. We're going to put you in your places tonight. We are taking a warring position. I believe it was Jeremiah who said if there's no bloodshed, there's no battle." A little boy wanders into the room. "Come on, Mohammed," McCloud calls, "join the men's team."

"You expect to get out of this alive?" asks one of the women as she crosses the room.

"All right," McCloud says. "The passage says that women should have coverings over their heads, that they shouldn't speak, that whatever they have to say should be said through their husbands. It says, first, that God made you as companions to men, and second, that you are supposed to be our helpmates. That's how I read it, and of course we're going to take the position that Paul is correct."

The women have a leader too, Maleika Mosley, a deacon at the church. "Taking the time into account?" she asks.

"Taking anything you want into account," McCloud replies with an expansive wave. He pulls the men into a huddle. "Hard-line Bible people would say that's right—and technically, we believe it," he tells them.

"Well, we believe it, but it depends," says one of his troops.

"Shh—don't talk so loud," McCloud says. "If they don't know that, we're not going to tell them tonight."

Across the room, Mosley is giving her team a quick introduction to the context of Corinthians: that pagan worship included phallic symbols, that pagan cults went after women just the way cults today go after the weakest members of the community; that men were the ones who were taught in the Jewish community, so women were forced to ask them for information.

"So women were subservient?" asks one woman.

"At that time," another adds quickly.

"You all ready?" taunts McCloud, really into his part.

"No."

"God have mercy, there's three of you to but one of us."

"All right," McCloud declares a moment later, "here's our beginning point, our central point, and we want to stand on that point all night. Go on, say it." He's been coaching Mohammed, who pipes his line on cue: "But woman is the glory of man."

"Prove it," demands a woman.

"It's in the Bible," McCloud smirks.

"But the last part of the chapter is 'it all comes from God.'"

"We're clear on that," McCloud responds, "but we want you to understand the order in which it comes from God. Woman came from man, and man from God."

"We all depend on each other," says one of the women.

"Where do you all get that equal stuff? That ain't in the Bible."

"But Paul was writing in a different time."

"But it's in the Bible."

McCloud's smug "it's in the Bible" both encapsulates and mocks an attitude I suspect these women have run into a good deal, and they're having trouble responding to it.

"Why did Paul write this?" one asks.

"There were two groups of people in this church and they were fussin'," says one of the men. "They were from two different backgrounds, and for them to have a common ground, Paul had to write this down."

Mosley begins making her case. "Paul wrote when two different nations existed—"

"Ooh, she's been to seminary," McCloud teases.

"The Greeks lived in a society where there was a lot of pagan worship, and pagan worshipers preyed on women."

McCloud explodes in mock wrath. "Is she calling us pagans?"

"The men were the ones that received the teaching and training," Mosley persists, "and the men were in the main sanctuary while the women were in the women's court."

"And why was that?" McCloud asks triumphantly. "You know why it was set up like that? An eleven-year-old boy can tell you. Go on, Mohammed, read it again."

"But woman is the glory of man."

"Yeah, but there were new times coming," Mosley argues, getting into her stride. "This is what Joel prophesied, that your sons *and daughters* will prophesy. The time where they would be equal would be coming in, but first women had to be brought into teaching, and to do that, men had to bring women in from being preyed upon."

"Who came first?" McCloud asks, referring to the story in Genesis of the creation of Eve from Adam's rib. "So who means most to God?"

"That's a coincidence," says a woman. "It's not to say the man means more."

"If you had to be part of a coincidence," McCloud retorts, "wouldn't you rather be part of a biblical coincidence?"

But women can make men, and men can't make women, argues one woman, prompting a debate over reproductive politics.

"All right," says one of the men, "we do live with women and we do need women to reproduce, but on the issue of protection, the issue of needing somebody to lead, you need men." He sounds like he's in earnest. "If someone breaks into the house, who are you going to send downstairs?"

"Me," says one of the women, to loud laughter.

"If the police come to the door, who are you going to want to protect you?"

"Depends on the police," she says, and gets another knowing laugh.

McCloud brings it to a close. "OK," he says, " there were major cultural issues concerned here, but I was amazed that you all bought into the second creation story. You bought it like I was selling hot candy. Why didn't someone think of the first, where God creates them at the same time?"

"I intentionally work to create tension," McCloud had told me that afternoon. "It spurs a great discussion. People who have been at Bible study longer can argue about how an issue makes them feel, and I really work at getting feelings." It seems to me, watching him, that McCloud is trying to develop in his students a freedom with the Bible that many of them do not have.

He turns to the second half of the chapter, where Paul discusses the Lord's Supper. "What could be an unworthy manner?" he asks.

"A clean heart, a clean mind," says one of the men.

"I hear you, but tell me what that really means."

Holding grudges, says one. Adultery, says another. "Thank you," says one of the women tartly; the sex war McCloud started earlier is still simmering.

Stealing, lying, being self-centered. "Give me an example," says McCloud.

"Well, if you're able to contribute to the church and you're not doing it."

Hatred, says another man. "Say another word about hatred," says McCloud.

"Well, say if I say I hate alcoholics," he says, "that would be wrong, but I could hate alcohol."

The first step in repentance is confession, McCloud says. "The Bible teaches that whatever you believe in your heart comes out of your mouth, so if you love money more than you love the Lord, don't say 'amen' when I preach like I did last Sunday. Any questions?"

Chapter 12

Church of St. Luke in the Fields

New York, NY

R oger Ferlo has been known to boast that the Church of St. Luke in the Fields, of which he is rector, has been offering Bible study on Monday nights for fifty years.

He exaggerates. I don't know about the '40s and '50s, but when I joined the parish in the '80s, there was no Bible study on Monday or any other night. Regular Bible study began about ten years ago. Since Ferlo's arrival five years later, the group has become a central feature of parish life, attracting anywhere from twenty-five to fifty people, not all of them parishioners or even Christians.

If I hadn't known Ferlo was an Episcopal priest when I first met him, I'd never have guessed. In a movie, he'd be cast not as the guy in the collar, but as his smart, sardonic sidekick: Frank Sinatra, not Bing Crosby; Spike Lee, not Denzel Washington. It was far easier for me to imagine him in a Yale classroom—where he was for several years a popular English professor—than behind the altar.

But Ferlo could not teach the Bible as he does, he told me when we talked about the class, if he weren't a priest. "It does bother me occasionally that I feel much more like my English-professor self than my priest self. On the other hand, we're only in the class because we're in the church. Unless it's linked to the sacramental life of the community, I have no business doing it. The fact that we gather around the altar is less a corrective to secular-sounding speculation about these texts than it is the grounding that allows us to talk about them.

"Biblical religion is a contradiction in terms," Ferlo said flatly. "If you think the Bible in and of itself is going to lead you to Jesus, you're on a fool's errand. It was never meant to be responded to in isolation. Unless your reading is embedded in the sacramental life, you may as well read Shakespeare; you will get more moral structure."

When Ferlo talks about the sacramental life of the community, he is dead serious; what brings people to St. Luke's and holds them there, more than anything else, is the Eucharist. Communion is a part of almost everything we do: weddings, funerals, healing services. At the end of many Sunday services, one or two laypeople are sent from the altar, carrying the consecrated bread and wine, to take it to housebound parishioners. Close to two hundred people—a third of the parish—participate one way or another: making vestments, arranging flowers, ironing linens, reading lessons, ushering, serving at the altar.

During the 11:15 service on Sundays, strangers often wander in, drawn by the music of Mozart or Josquin des Pres or Arvo Pärt. I'll watch them occasionally, wondering what they make of it: the incense, the processions, the singing of everything that can possibly be sung. It is out of a different age; when Ferlo, sitting in the enormous carved and inlaid celebrant's chair behind the altar, clothed in brocade vestments, rests his chin in his hand, he looks for all the world like Michelangelo's statue of Lorenzo de Medici, in Florence's Medici Chapel.

Like any deep passion, our enthusiasm for liturgy has its ridiculous side. We happily debate arcane questions; a recent argument concerned the proper liturgical color to use in frosting the cupcakes for the Feast of St. Mary the Virgin. But these are frills; at its core, the splendor and the sensuality of our worship speaks to us, however faintly and haltingly, of the splendor of God.

The same is true of Bible study. However much it may resemble a college seminar (one member, an atheist, says that's why he

comes—it's a free college education), most of us are there
because we believe that in some way, this book too speaks to us
of God. "If I can get people to think of themselves as in a relationship with scripture," Ferlo said to me once, "there is a chance
they can recognize a relationship with God when they meet one."

We've read a lot on Monday nights: Gospels, Genesis, Isaiah,
Job, the books of Samuel and Kings, Q material. We have gone
over the first draft of Ferlo's book, *Opening the Bible,* as well as
a work in progress, on the Bible and the senses. About half the
parish, and thus the Bible study, is gay; early in his tenure, Ferlo
spent several months taking an edgy group through the letters of
Paul, trying (with considerable success) to introduce them to an
apostle who didn't erect boundaries, but smashed them.

About fifty people are crowded into the meeting room for the
first night of a six-week study of the book of Revelation—twenty
more than the room holds comfortably. People perch on tables
and counters—wherever they can find a spot.

To many of us, and certainly to me, Revelation speaks more of
subway-handout craziness than it does of God. (One Monday
night regular—a retired priest—went on strike till we'd done
with the book. "It's not edifyin'," he complained.) A vivid and violent vision of plague, destruction, and the grandeur of heaven,
Revelation barely made it into the Bible and is hardly ever read
in mainstream churches. But it is also the source of much of the
church's imagery of worship—and the happy hunting ground of
end-of-the-world theorists like Hal Lindsey and Pat Robertson.

Ferlo walks in laden with even more handouts than usual—a
show-and-tell of commentaries, charts, samples of apocalyptic
writing. The first thing he wants us to realize is that this book is
not unique. There was a lot of apocalyptic, or end-of-the-world
writing, floating around in the centuries just before and after the
death of Christ. There's a lot of it in the Bible itself: in Mark, in
Daniel. "It was in the air," he says. "Those who heard Revelation
were already steeped in the rhetoric and method of apocalyptic."

But we're not. So the first evening is devoted to learning the
code. Ferlo hands out a chart that translates the numerological

symbolism with which Revelation is packed: 666, the sign of the beast; the 144,000 saved; the seven churches and the seven bowls and the seven lamp stands. "Four is universality; six is imperfection; seven is completion, perfection. The whole logic of the storytelling is in sevens—sevens inside sevens."

"*Seven Brides for Seven Brothers,*" mutters Dorothy.

Ferlo jumps on it. "That's helpful. That's the level on which we're dealing. It's just a given. All right, twelve. Guess what, there were twelve tribes of Israel. And why are there 144,000 saved? Well, surprise, surprise, it's a factor of twelve. And a thousand means a lot, so a thousand thousand is a lot of lots, and 144,000 is not only a lot, but a factor of twelve, so it's a *significant* lot. OK? We're not counting heads—we're reading Revelation. This is how you think."

I have been waiting eagerly for this class, because Revelation both bewilders and irritates me. Of all the books in the Bible, it is the one that seems to me to give the most backing to those who believe God is just waiting to zap all the sinners who haven't accepted Christ as their personal savior. "How long, oh Lord, how long," ask the souls of the martyrs in heaven, and in answer God sends his angels, and the four horsemen of the Apocalypse, to pour terror on the earth. Reading Revelation, you can understand the appeal of the peculiar (and only faintly biblical) theory of the rapture—that those who have accepted Christ will be whisked away into heaven before the end of the world comes. I'd want to be whisked out of this mess too.

"This was probably a quite sophisticated, hellenized Jewish culture," Ferlo says the following week, of the culture in which—and to counter which—Revelation was written. To those easygoing, hellenized Jews, the community that produced this book looked like a bunch of fanatics. They were a lot more like the subway preachers we tend to shrink from, than they were like us.

We get a lot of Greek on Monday nights. "The Greek word translated 'revelation' is *apocalypsis,*" Ferlo says. "'Revelation' is a calm translation. What it's talking about is blowing the lid off— blowing the lid off things as they seem, so we may see them as they are."

That's exactly what Ferlo tries to do in Bible study, where "bracket" often seems to be his favorite word. He says it over and over: "Bracket your assumptions about what this text is saying." Most readers, he told me, think a book is a book is a book. The idea that writers had strategies, and that there are different rules for reading different kinds of texts, is strange to them. "When you add to that the sacredness of the Bible, and the sense that it is a unitary monument, that's a big leap. It's not an easy thing I ask when I tell people to please bracket what they think they know."

But only when you set aside what you know can the surprises come. Richard Bentley, a regular, though mostly silent, class member, told me about his amazement when we read Matthew's nativity story. "To me, it stood as it was. But when we read it, there was one sentence that I had never seen. I had never realized that Joseph went through all the horrors that a man would go through who found out his wife was pregnant. And then to finally realize that he adopted the pure Jewish idea of forgiving her and accepting her and giving the child a name. I had passed right over all that, to where the angel comes and says everything is OK. Talk about being hit in the face with something."

We don't go through the biblical books line by line. Rather, Ferlo will choose chunks of text to pick apart, modeling the techniques so that we can begin to use them ourselves. Right now, he's parsing the titles the author uses for Jesus in the first chapter: "the faithful witness, the firstborn of the dead, and ruler of the kings of the earth."

"From the Greek word witness, we get the word martyr," he says. "He's calling Jesus the faithful martyr and what else? First begotten from the dead. Well, first begotten means there's going to be a tenth begotten and a hundredth and a 144,000th. Then ruler of the kings of the earth. That was Caesar's title, and this community is saying it's Jesus' title. See what I mean by radical writing?"

"He's asserting that Jesus is God," volunteers Vince, "but he hasn't joined the Trinity. He's still distinct."

"You're trying to do it as logic," Ferlo says. "Here's another way. This section opens with a description of God, at the center is a description of Christ, and at the end is a description of God.

It's a God sandwich—you start with God, go to Jesus, and can't go back to God except with Jesus. It's theology in motion. We're right at the root of Christian theology."

I spent several years in Ferlo's Bible study before I realized just why I found it so exciting—and the person who made it clear to me wasn't Ferlo, but a Berkeley professor of Hebrew and comparative literature named Robert Alter. We used Alter's annotated translation when we studied Genesis, and I found his footnotes so entertaining that I bought, and read, his 1981 book on reading scripture.

It was, for me, a revelation—a missing-my-subway-stop page turner. His argument is summed up in his book's title: *The Art of Biblical Narrative.* It sounds self-evident. Whatever else they think it is, most people regard the Bible as a Great Book. If it's a great book, of course its narrative is artful.

But to somebody brought up, as I had been, on historical-biblical criticism, it was an explosive theory. In college I had been taught (by Ursula Niebuhr, no less) that to talk about the author of a biblical book was sheer naivete. These documents were amalgams, things of shreds and patches, pulled together by some anonymous soul who—fortunately for scholars—hadn't even managed to hide the seams. If something in a biblical book seemed strange, the answer was obvious—it had come from some entirely different document, and had been plugged in there because the redactor (to use the technical term) had been either too careless, or too reverent toward anything that came out of his sacred tradition, to rewrite the passage so it made sense.

Alter, who came to the Bible almost accidentally in an academic career devoted primarily to modern European and English literature, but has since become one of its prominent modern translators, pours scorn on that approach. "Academic Bible study has asked questions which are in themselves important," he said to me when I called to talk about his book. "But historical conjectures take us away from reading the text. If you're trying to figure out exactly where each component of text that you think you can identify comes from, you're not at all reading the text. Even if the stories were put together, they were put together with a sense of purpose."

Alter's assumption, then, is that the text, as we have it on the page, is trying to have an effect on its readers. And if you look carefully at how it is working, you can see what it's trying to do. In particular, Alter says, look for surprises: places where the text does not follow the patterns that it has already set you up to expect. Often, these are the sections of scripture that scholars call interpolations. In the story of Joseph, for instance, Joseph's brothers discover twice that the money they paid for grain has somehow reappeared in their sacks. Logically, Alter says, that makes no sense, and so scholars have assumed that two versions of the story have been clumsily cobbled together.

The writer was not so stupid, Alter argues; illogical though it may be, the double occurrence makes perfect narrative sense. He compares it to a film montage: the two versions play against each other, enriching the story by providing different information and different perspectives. The result, he says, is an "effect of multifaceted truth."

For literary scholars, this kind of analysis is nothing new—this is how literature works. For biblical scholarship, it is a revolution. A revolution in more ways than one, because it offers a way of reading that, at least in its simplest forms, anybody can learn. "I have presented some of these ideas even to high school students," Alter told me. "If you show them how things are repeated almost verbatim, then you can show how a little swerve from verbatim to nonverbatim opens up a new perspective. Once you walk people through one or two stories where it's done, they can do it themselves."

I had that brought home to me one night in the Genesis Bible study. We were working on Abraham's sacrifice of Isaac, a story I had read often, and always with deep discomfort. Most of us, in fact, squirmed at Abraham's unquestioning obedience to God's outrageous command—and at the narrator's apparent approval of that obedience.

Armed by Alter, though, I noticed that night that when Abraham leads Isaac to the sacrifice, the narrator—who has up until now given us only enough dialogue to advance the plot—sud-

denly gives us a conversation that, from a plot point of view, is
entirely unnecessary:

> Abraham took the wood of the burnt offering and laid it on
> his son Isaac, and he himself carried the fire and the knife.
> So the two of them walked on together. Isaac said to his
> father Abraham, "Father!" And he said, "Here I am, my
> son." He said, "The fire and the wood are here, but where
> is the lamb for a burnt offering?" Abraham said, "God him-
> self will provide the lamb for a burnt offering, my son." So
> the two of them walked on together.

By using the words "father" and "son" every chance he gets,
he seems to be rubbing our noses in the horrifying unnaturalness
of this act. Maybe, I began to think, my discomfort with this story
was not rebellion against God, or incomprehension of the
ancient Hebrew moral viewpoint—two of the solutions I had
been offered. Maybe I was *supposed* to be uncomfortable.
Maybe this narrator's moral stance was a lot more complex than
I had realized.

That's the kind of reading that Ferlo is trying to teach as well.
"I believe that accepting a plurality of visions enlarges you and
enlarges the text," he told me. "To ignore the words, and the play
of words, and playfulness of the words, and the myriad of
words—to ignore the generative energy of those words—is to
ignore the Bible."

While we were working on the story of Joseph at St. Luke's, I
was hearing the same story explicated by the BOLD preachers,
whose approach was to mine the text for religious meaning and
spiritual lessons. We didn't get any of that on Monday nights, and
I asked Ferlo why not.

It was a deliberate decision, he said. "I didn't do much with
the religious implications of the Joseph story because I wanted
people to understand its complexity and texture. If they can't do
that, then they have no right to the other implications. If they're
tone-deaf to the way in which it unfolds, the way in which the

language works, its resonance to other stories, then for me, they have no theological standing."

The words on the page matter, he said. "There is no one single person whose intention has made the Bible the coherent document that it is. No single person, but an entire culture. And I, being a religious reader, would say that, as it was a culture that was God-shaped, so the language is God-shaped."

"We're going to do some Bible jumping," Ferlo announces in the following week's Revelation class. He starts with the great scene of heaven in chapter 4: God seated on the throne surrounded by twenty-four elders, flaming torches, and four living creatures full of eyes, and around it all a sea of glass.

"This is gorgeous stuff," he says, "and he didn't make it up. Go to Second Corinthians. This is where Dante got his whole Divine Comedy." He's citing the passage where Paul, laying claim to visions and revelations, describes a vision of the third heaven, where he heard "things that are not to be told."

"Even Paul's vision, its highest ecstasy, is itself reminiscent of a prophetic vision," Ferlo tells us. "Skip again, to Ezekiel 1. 'As I looked, a great cloud, with brightness around it and fire flashing forth, and in the middle of the fire, gleaming amber. Four living creatures, darting to and fro, like lightning.' Without Ezekiel, chapter 4 of Revelation wouldn't have been written."

Ferlo jumps around the Bible as much as any conservative teacher, but he's looking for something different. They're looking for facts and doctrines that they can put into a consistent whole. Ferlo is looking not for consistency, but for what he described to me as a "deep convergence—capital D, capital C." He is trying to give us a sense of the biblical conversation: the constant interplay among the book's writers.

"There are deep biblical precedents for the vision of John's revelation," he tells us now. "What we're seeing is not a crazy invention by a demented or pot-smoking evangelist. What we're seeing is a canny, shrewd, brilliant, visionary assimilation of the Old Testament prophetic visions, and a transmuting of them, into visions not of God the Father, but of the Lamb at the center of the throne."

He talks us, word by word, through the moment when the vision of God dissolves, like a movie, into something utterly new. "Who is worthy to open the scroll? No one in heaven or earth or under the earth. Then one of the elders said to me, 'No, don't weep, *watch.*' The dissolve is about to happen. 'See, the Lion of the tribe of Judah, the root of David has conquered.' And in the very next verse—'I saw a Lamb.' The lion has become a lamb and the lamb is on the throne. Talk about wild—the image is absurd. Who's going to worship a slaughtered lamb? But guess what? Chapters 4 and 5 went to the very center of every act of Christian worship. We are overhearing the notes, the tones, the nuances, the language of the very earliest form of Christian worship."

"When I'm teaching the Bible," Ferlo told me, "I am perpetually stuck in English 101. Before you go anywhere, you have to learn how to read, with this kind of attention, which for me is a lot more attention than either liberals or conservatives tend to give these texts. A lot of Bible readers are very well-intentioned, but ill-trained. There is a discipline of reading—you have to learn the protocols. Reading the Bible with a fifth-grade sensibility is not always innocuous."

Next week, he's going to put new demands on our attention. He's going to be away, and while he's gone, he wants us to try an experiment. "I want to enlist you to go into the church and sit in the dark, with a couple of candles burning, and hear the whole thing. This book was meant to be experienced all at once, by the community, in a sacred space. Are you game for that?"

Not all of us are, it turns out; only about half the group turns up the following week. Candlelight is insufficient, so the readers finally drag out a standing lamp. In the soft, sharply angled light, the seven readers, most of whom I know well by daylight, take on the aura of figures on a Vermeer canvas.

Ferlo talks a lot about how we've lost the ability to listen, and as the reading begins, I quickly realize he's right. My thoughts wander. Odd things, like the measures of wheat and barley for a day's pay, catch my attention and bewilder me. I wonder idly whether John's fractions add up. After a while, I begin to notice that what pulls my attention back to the text isn't the beatific vision of the lamb, the heavenly city. It's the plagues, the violence, the pit of fire, the war and destruction.

The week before, I had been swept away by Ferlo's passionate evocation of the vision of the Lamb on the throne. But now, I feel as though I'm listening to a demented television weatherman: earthquakes, stars falling to earth and turning water to wormwood, scorching heat, black darkness, hundred-pound hailstones. No wonder subway evangelists make such hay with Revelation. This is powerful, deeply unpleasant stuff.

Bentley, one of our seven readers, told me afterwards that he would need to hear the book several times more to really understand it. "I understand the concepts of the good and evil spirits out there, and Michael driving Satan into hell. But did I comprehend it all? No. It amazes me to listen to fundamentalists, who can pick it apart as though it makes sense. To me it's like some weird nightmare."

When we come back together the following week, we talk a lot about imagery. The woman clothed with the sun carries resonances not only of Hebrew and Christian culture, but of pagan culture as well, Ferlo says. "If you go to Rome, and go way down below the Vatican to the pagan necropolis, you'll be shown something that was uncovered in the late Middle Ages and so scandalized them that it wasn't uncovered again until the modern era. It's an early Christian tomb with an image of the sun god Apollo as Christ. That's the same kind of sensibility going on here. You take a pagan image, and destroy it and redeem it at the same time.

"Who is this male child who's going to rule all the nations with a rod of iron?" he asks us, sending us to Psalm 2 for the answer. "You shall break them with a rod of iron," he reads. "If you were a first-century Asia Minor Christian, you wouldn't have to look it up. This writer had at his fingertips an immense store of cultural apparatus by which to explain what he later calls a mystery—that which cannot be explained but which must be explained."

"He must have been incredibly scholarly," says Valerie.

"No, we're scholarly," says Ferlo. "He had it in his head." He puzzles over how to get this across. "Here—'Oh, say can you see . . .' what comes into your head?"

"By the dawn's early light," we chorus.

"It's part of his mental furniture. Do we have that kind of cultural patrimony?"

We come up with images from advertising, superstitions, slang, marketing.

"But if the question is how to make sense of who Jesus is in our own imagery and language in such a powerful and evocative way . . ." asks Dorothy.

"We have a community here that uses this imagery every Sunday," Ferlo responds.

"In some ways, it's talking about how to describe what's truly horrible," says Bob. "And in Bosnia it's happening right now."

"It's different from Bosnia," I say. "God's not doing that, people are. But in Revelation, God's doing it."

"And that's bad?" Ferlo asks.

"Well, it makes me dreadfully uncomfortable."

"Maybe it's akin to our understanding not being able to encompass all of God," says Ian. "It's a working-out of what is to happen, but we don't have a sense of the guy up there doing it. There isn't a sense of a puppeteer."

"The image I have is of a judge," says Nelson, "somebody sitting there and watching the whole movie."

"Look at verse 9," says Maggie. "Fire came down from heaven and consumed them and they will be tormented day and night forever and ever." This is not God's self-sacrificing crucifixion, she argues; this is vengeance.

"Yeah," says Ferlo, "but it's also myth. I guess for me—and I might be wrong in this—the rules of the game, in reading this, are that those who are wrong, are wrong."

"It seems like the antithesis of Christ," says Jack.

"I understand that. But it's in the Bible. And the Christ of the Gospels isn't meek and mild. When he says turn the other cheek, it's a challenge."

"But that sort of severity is of a different order than casting enemies into the fire," argues Ian.

"God, you're really tough on these people," Ferlo exclaims. "This is how they're imagining it. And it's the powers of evil being tossed out."

"But there are people that are the earthly incarnation of these evil powers, right? People like Nero that we can spell out, we can identify."

"We're really at the cusp of this," Ferlo says, "because this definitely is a community, or at least a writer, who will say, 'Look, folks, are you going to be lukewarm about this? Then I will spit you out.' Because what's at stake? There were people in the French Resistance who said that."

What's at stake is a question we've gotten from Ferlo over and over. It's one of his techniques for recognizing, and coping with, the foreignness of the Bible. If we can see what is at stake for the communities out of which it came, perhaps we can find some points of connection. It doesn't seem to be working well tonight, and Ferlo takes a deep breath before trying once again. "The text bothers you? Sorry, deal with it," he'd said to me once. "Don't walk away or make it say something it doesn't say." Dealing with it is usually easier than this, though. Tonight it feels as though this text is a grindstone, and he's holding our faces to it.

"Who would *not* want death and Hades to be tossed into the lake of fire?" he asks.

"There's a difference between eradicating them and torturing them for all time,"says Maggie.

Ferlo buries his head in his arms. "We're talking about *death,* man. I don't need the smallpox virus or the HIV virus to be around. I want it gone, out, dead."

"But there's a difference between gone and tortured."

"I'm amazed," he says. "So death is OK. Look, verse 14: death and Hades were thrown into the lake of fire."

"But there really are people who polarize others as evil," says Ian.

"I grant you that," Ferlo responds. "And I find that wholesale condemnation impossible. But what the theology of this book is saying is that in Christ, evil—however we imagine or embody it—is defeated. Sure, there is a gray area where people who are evil might be redeemed. But that's not what this is about."

The next week—our last week with this book—Ferlo tries to make some connections. "How does our experience of evil in the late twentieth century correspond with the experience of this community?" he asks us. "Are we so removed from them that this book has nothing to say to us?"

The question sets off a furious debate—not so much with him, as with each other. There are at least a dozen different theological viewpoints bouncing back and forth.

"Hitler and the Holocaust are perceived as a form of evil unique to us," says Jack.

"That's an easy one," says Ferlo, pushing it. "What about the carpet bombing of North Vietnam, where we are implicit? Some of the religious figures in the antiwar movement would say Vietnam was one of the evil powers of the world that we need to renounce."

"Or the American Indians," says Bob, our most determinedly political regular.

"Revelation talks about evil from the point of view of someone who has not participated in it," I say. "What help is that to us who have participated, and do, and know that we do?"

"That's how fundamentalists read the whole book," says Thomas, who comes from a fundamentalist background. "They're the untouched people, and the rest of us are going to hell in a handbasket."

No, no, no, says Cindy, who has been waving her arms in frustration at our blindness. The book is about repentance, she insists; we are *supposed* to identify with the sinners who get zapped. "They're like us. They're hiding out in crags, and who can stand? Who can *not* identify with that? He keeps saying, 'repent, repent,' but he doesn't cut off the Christian hope, because we get a vision of the people already in heaven."

I think she's sweetening the book. "People get zapped, and they don't repent, so they get zapped again," I argue. "But there doesn't seem to be any serious consideration of the possibility that they might repent."

Ferlo agrees with me—for different reasons. It's like Exodus, he says; "The story would not work if the pharaoh repented."

"Somebody's got to get judged," says John. "I'm not going to take that power from God."

Wait a minute, says Jack. "This book wasn't written by the community—it was a dream that John had. Revelation warns me about the evil in me and tells me I have to do something about it."

"But how does that help the people in Hiroshima?" asks Bob. "If it says the good will be rewarded—well, for millions, that's not true."

"Right," says Ferlo, "which is why Jack is moving it away from a political perspective to a personal and moral perspective."

Nelson, who has all along insisted that the book raises false hopes, chimes in here. "Is the purpose of reading and studying the Bible to help us lead a Christian life within ourselves and the world? Even though we die and that's it?"

"I was facing a dilemma as to whether this was fact or fiction," Nelson Colòn told me after the class was over. "I was brought up Seventh-Day Adventist, and Revelation was *the* book."

Ferlo takes up his challenge. "The gospel speaks of more than a way of living," he responds. "It's said here in a different way, but it's what Paul was convinced of and Jesus was convinced of and Christians are convinced of: that in death, God does not separate himself from us. When Paul got pressed to say what it looks like, feels like, he couldn't do it—but the Easter experience was that even though death is, death is not."

"The problem I have is believing that."

"Right, that's the act of faith. But for the Gospel writers, the way of living stems from this conviction. It's because we are resurrected people that we live our lives in this way—not if we live our lives in this way, everything will be OK."

"Well, the reason I do Bible study," says Bob, "is to know God, and why God does the things he does through Christ. I never get any answers."

The class ends in a burst of laughter.

Getting answers is not what this class is about. Revelation is still an enigma for him, Colòn told me. "But I am able now to understand the book within its context. It doesn't hang over me the way it did."

Maggie Robbins, who had pointed out the vengeance in Revelation, told me that she learned when she walked in the door that we don't deal in answers. As a new member of the church, she had heard a lot about the Bible study; she had also studied Shakespeare with Ferlo at Yale. "I wanted to go, but I assumed it was very, very learned. I thought it must be all these really smart, really old people."

The day she finally turned up, we were reading the odd story, in the Gospel of Mark, of the fig tree. Jesus is hungry, and goes looking for figs out of season; when he doesn't find them, he curses the tree and it withers.

"I thought the Bible was going to make sense," she said. "But this story had no moral purpose, and when I asked about it, no one could help me at all. I thought 'Oh, this is much weirder than I thought.'"

Like most religious readers, Robbins came to the Bible looking for instruction about leading a Christian life. "I went three years in this church struggling with the Beatitudes," she said. "I was bummed, because I thought—these people were blessed, so what was I going to do? It didn't occur to me until I was reading Huxley that the challenge was to become what they are." Whatever the Bible is about, she went on, it's not instruction. "That's a lot easier to find in Lao Tse. He wrote straight at you. But even Zen koans are not as crazy as parables. Parables are off the wall."

The instinct to read the Bible for the meaning we expect to find is as strong among us as it is in any group of Bible readers. Robbins has become a Bible study regular, helping to organize a parishioner-led group in the summer when the regular class takes a break. She told me about a discussion of Paul's letter to the Corinthians that reminded me of the discussion I'd heard at Precept Ministries. "Several people said, 'This is *St. Paul.* Everything he said is what we must attempt.'"

"Then half of us [the female half] can't talk," Robbins responded, "because we're in a church building."

The women in Chattanooga, though, sounded to me like high school students arguing with the principal, using all their ingenuity to get around somebody else's rules. As those of us in the Monday night group have learned, you read the Bible very differently when you consider yourself part of the community that wrote it.

"They said, 'Oh, no, not the part about women preaching,'" Robbins told me. "'The other part.' Well, which part? And who gets to pick? I'm fascinated by what was chosen and what wasn't and whether it's going to change. Roger has this thing about the Bible being a living, breathing document because we enter into discussion with the people who wrote it."

What Robbins seems to find in the Bible is not a guide, but a picture. "When people corner Jesus and ask him what's the most important commandment," she told me, "he says, 'Love one another as I love you.' Well, if you look at how he loved them, it means be tough, upbraid people, and pay them a lot of attention. There isn't much that's sweet about it."

John Merz, who'd refused to deny God the right to judge in the Revelation class, told me that for him, to be a Christian is to live in two worlds. "You're called to be a complete citizen of your time, but when you start to engage the tradition of scripture, now you're also a citizen of the last two thousand years at least. You're automatically not only multicultural, but multiepochal, too.

"Sometimes," Merz told me, "if I'm pushing really hard to understand, say, the community Paul was writing to, a flag will go up, and I realize that however much I take apart scripture, I am never going to pin down in some way exactly who God is or how God is in the world." But if it doesn't give answers, he said, "it has a power to question every corner of your life."

St. Luke's is the community in which I read the Bible, and it's hard for me to stand apart from it to assess its effect, on me or on anybody else. But I know why I keep coming back to Bible study, week after week, despite times—sometimes whole evenings—of tedium, irritation, and frustration. I come for those moments when something hits me in a way I had not expected and opens my imagination to a new glimpse, a new facet, of God. It happened the night, in Genesis, that I realized the narrator wasn't as single-minded as I'd thought, and suddenly there was room in this community for my discomfort, too. It happened again during our fierce debates over Revelation, as we kicked the words and images of Revelation around the room like a soccer ball, and I knew that we, and the author of this book, and his community, were—for all our disagreements—in this thing together.

Jesus talked about giving his followers streams of living water; well, at their best, Monday nights leave me feeling I've been given not water, but champagne. When I walk out, my soul is bubbling and slightly off-kilter, as though I am responding, at least for a little while, to an entirely different form of gravity.

Conclusion

A couple of years ago, I was invited up to Union Theological Seminary for a retirement party for Robin Scroggs, a well-liked professor of biblical theology. Academia being what it is, the party proper was preceded by a panel discussion on the authority of the Bible. And Union being what *it* is, the panelists didn't, by and large, think the Bible has any.

What stuck in my memory, though, was a remark Scroggs made quite early in the discussion. "I think there would be a certain freedom if we gave up the text as authority," he said. "It would no longer be a club to hit other people over the head; people wouldn't think their faith position depended on proving they were right and the other side was wrong; it would increase the interest of people in synagogues and churches in the matters that scripture addresses. It would be a lot more fun."

There's something very appealing about Scroggs's vision of a world in which, instead of battling over the Bible, we all sit around a table and discuss it like gentlefolk. But the more I watched people struggling with this book, the more I realized that his vision was based on an assumption that may be possible only in an academic setting: that reading the Bible can be fun. The Bible, fun?

208

For most of the people I met, both liberal and conservative, the Bible, taken raw, is no fun at all. It is a deeply off-putting book.

And what's more, they're right.

"The Bible is without question one of the most unsatisfying books ever written," wrote Thomas Merton, in an introduction to a Time-Life Books edition of the Bible that never came to fruition. "It is of the very nature of the Bible to affront, perplex and astonish the human mind. Hence the reader who opens the Bible must be prepared for disorientation, confusion, incomprehension, perhaps outrage."

Those are not emotions that most of us enjoy laying ourselves open to. Particularly not, as Merton went on to point out, if the book that is causing those emotions is the one we are taught by our religious tradition to describe as the word of God. That charged phrase means different things to different people, certainly, but I think almost all of its meanings carry some sense of the Bible as a vehicle for meeting God. And faced with a God who is, in Merton's terms, disorienting, confusing, incomprehensible, and outrageous, we start to squirm.

As I watched people study the Bible, I often felt that what I was witnessing was more than anything else an exercise in damage control. The Bible, in all its raw messiness, seemed to be at least as much of a threat as a gift. Like some uncomfortable political scandal, it had to be kept, at all costs, from erupting.

There are a lot of ways of managing the Bible, but the most common, at least among religious people, is to run it through a theological filter: to declare, up front, that the Bible is a road map to heaven, or a user-friendly operator's manual, or the action plan for God's domination-free order. Liberals hang their hats on the Gospels and the prophets, dodge a lot of the epistles, and run screaming from Revelation; conservatives flip the image upside down. Each camp insists that it has the true picture.

And the trouble is, they're both right. The Bible is all of that and more; it won't fit through anyone's theological filter. It is too huge: not just in size, although its size alone is formidable, but in breadth and scope and in theology.

Just look at the book of Genesis, which begins with not one, but two creation stories. In the first one, God commands the world into existence out of nothing. He brings into being the firmament, the seas, the plants and animals by the sheer power of his word, and finally, on the sixth day, creates man and woman to rule what he has made. This God is cosmic and mysterious, a being of absolute power, who has no need of personality.

The second story seems to be about an entirely different God, one who kneels on the ground and shapes a man out of the mud, then digs into his body to make a woman out of his rib. This is an almost human God, a God who can be upset and angry. This God wanders the Garden of Eden looking for Adam, but can't find him because he's hiding; and when this God sends Adam and Eve out of the garden, he makes garments for them.

The theological counterpoint continues throughout the Bible. The detail-obsessed God of the books of Deuteronomy and Leviticus, whose rules cover every aspect of life—from the grandeur of the Ten Commandments to the designs on the hems of the priests' robes—is countered by the outraged God of the prophets, who despises a theology that puts worship ahead of justice and mercy. The God who wants to be Israel's only ruler is balanced by the God who chooses David and builds him a glorious kingdom. The prim-and-proper God of many of the later books of the Old Testament, which insist that the person who behaves properly will prosper (the Hebrew version of the evangelicals' "name it and claim it" theology), meets more than his match in the unaccountable and mysterious God of the book of Job, who scathingly attacks those who, like Job's comforters, have the temerity to claim they're explaining his ways. Even the New Testament, written over a much briefer period of time to tell a single story, first tells it four different ways, and then interprets it, in the epistles, from multiple and often conflicting angles. "There are some things in them hard to understand," says the writer of the second letter of Peter about the letters of Paul, "which the ignorant and unstable twist to their own destruction, as they do the other scriptures."

"Why does God have to be so confusing?" asked my husband, half seriously, on the way home from Bible study one night. "Why can't he just say what he means?"

Well, one answer to that question is that the Bible is not God's declaration to us; it is God's conversation with us. And conversations are convoluted things. They go around in circles; they tack from side to side; they make great leaps of logic and then loop back to a place that's not quite where they started. They attempt breathtaking jumps over great gaps of misunderstanding, sometimes landing safely on the other side and sometimes smashing up utterly on the rocks of confusion.

If all of that is true of a conversation even between two people, the complexities are compounded when more voices get into the act. Well, the voices in the Bible are legion. This book has existed, in one form or another, for thousands of years, and the conversations reflected in it have been joined, since then, by readers of every culture and nation under the heavens.

The great gift of the writers of the Bible, I have come to believe, is that they anticipated this. They knew that God speaks in many voices, and as they edited and commented on the work of earlier writers, they took care not to erase those voices in the process of adding their own. The writer who edited the story of David, from exile in Babylon, left the glory of the monarchy still visible through his queasy second thoughts. The writer who combined several sources into the book of Genesis didn't choose a single creation story but embraced both. And when the early Christian church undertook the most far-reaching reimagining of scripture of all—turning the Jewish scriptures into nothing more than an elaborate and prophetic preface to the story of Jesus—it included in its Bible, unchanged, the Jewish writings it had so comprehensively reinterpreted.

I am not arguing that to read the Bible properly, we must inhabit its every last nook and corner. We can't. The Bible's variety seems to be more than the human mind can compass; few readers in any age have been able to embrace it fully. For all of us, there are parts of the Bible that speak to us and parts that don't—places where, as Ferlo put it, we will not let the book take us and places where we have to let it take us.

But I do believe that to let the Bible speak anything at all new to us, we need to find a way of reading that holds in balance its integrity and our own. And to do that, we need to wrestle with the question Scroggs and his colleagues were addressing that evening at Union: the question of biblical authority. To read the Bible with integrity, we need in some way to answer the question, "Who's in charge here?"

Far more than interpretation, this is the subject on which conservatives and liberals are at loggerheads. That's why Scroggs's remark seemed to me both so wistful and so wrongheaded. Put liberals and conservatives in the same room to talk about this subject, and there would be no gentility on view at all. It would be a free-for-all, like those afternoon TV talk shows where everybody starts by screaming and is soon trading blows.

For conservatives, the Bible is in charge: beyond argument, beyond question, beyond objection. When, in *Mother Jones,* I described reading the Bible as a dialogue, not a monologue, a conservative journal came down on me like a ton of bricks. By what authority, its editors asked, did I decide what in the Bible to accept and what to reject, if not by that very truth it accused me of disdaining?

Liberals take the opposite tack. For them, the Bible is whatever the reader makes of it: not a source of truth, but a taking-off place in the search for truth beyond it. It provides the raw material of theories and visions without measure. But, in itself, it is ephemeral, shape-shifting, lacking not just authority but almost any kind of solid existence.

There has got, I kept thinking, to be a better way. And for me, at least, what that way might be is hinted at in the two very different Bible studies that end this book. The members of the two groups have little in common. The folks at First A.M.E. are down-to-earth; inclined, I think, to be literal-minded; and still a bit uncertain of their right to argue, either with the Bible or with McCloud. The members of the St. Luke's group, particularly those of us who do most of the talking, are intense, self-consciously intellectual, and reluctant even for a moment to cede our right to challenge anyone about anything.

What the two groups have in common, though, is that both look at the Bible not as they want it to be, or not to be, or as they have always been taught it was, but as it is, in its rawness, there on the page in front of them.

There is no substitute, I came to believe, for the words themselves. So often, as I watched people talk about the Bible, I felt that they were talking not about the book itself, with all its multitudinous voices, but about an iconic image that had no voice at all. Shortly after I came back from Colorado Springs, I saw in the Sunday paper an ad for the latest offering from the Franklin Mint: a china Bible. Even apart from the headline ("The Word of the Lord") on the ad, you could tell it was the Bible; it was a fat book with gilded pages, and it was open to a picture of a rather grim-looking Jesus, accompanied by a quote from John's Gospel. That was it, I thought; that was the Bible I had been seeing: an open book that you cannot actually read, because though the pages are replicated in careful detail, you can't turn them.

It is in turning the pages—reading the words—that we are able to begin to recognize and address the relationship between our own experience and understanding of God, and the experience and understanding of those who wrote those words and those who have read them before. It is the tension between the need to take the book seriously and the need to take ourselves seriously that makes the cracks that let God through.

At one point during my biblical arguments with Earl Jackson, he turned to me and asked, in what I think was genuine bewilderment, "Then what authority *does* the Bible have for you?" I hadn't ever considered the question before and had to think a long time before I could come up with any answer at all. "That it's there," I finally said. "That I have to deal with it."

The Bible, read faithfully, is never going to be entirely clear, entirely manageable, or entirely safe. Like the God it describes, it is itself a mystery: baffling, evasive, sometimes frightening, and charged, like a thundercloud, with a truth that can be recognized, but never explained.

Peter Gomes calls the book—borrowing a phrase from Thomas Cranmer—the lively oracles of God. That's the title he would choose for his biblical interpretation class at Harvard, he said, "if it wouldn't induce derision in the registrar's office."

While I was in Cambridge, I sat in on the last meeting of that class and listened to Gomes talking to his students about oracles. "What is the nature of an oracle?" he asked. "An oracle is a source of wisdom in which you place some implicit trust even if you don't understand the nature of the wisdom the oracle gives you. An oracle is all-seeing, all-knowing, and to some degree all-powerful. But the peculiar dynamic of an oracle is that its response to questioners is never direct, never explicit, always with the kind of ambiguity that it's incumbent on the questioner to interpret and develop. The nature of what an oracle says is a truth that can't be easily tacked down, and that is not subject in advance to the sovereignty of facts."

For me, as for Gomes and Cranmer, that's as good a picture as any of what it is to be faithful both to the Bible and to ourselves. Take it and read.

Index

215